Making
SCRAP QUILTS
TO USE IT UP!

D0492379

David and Charles

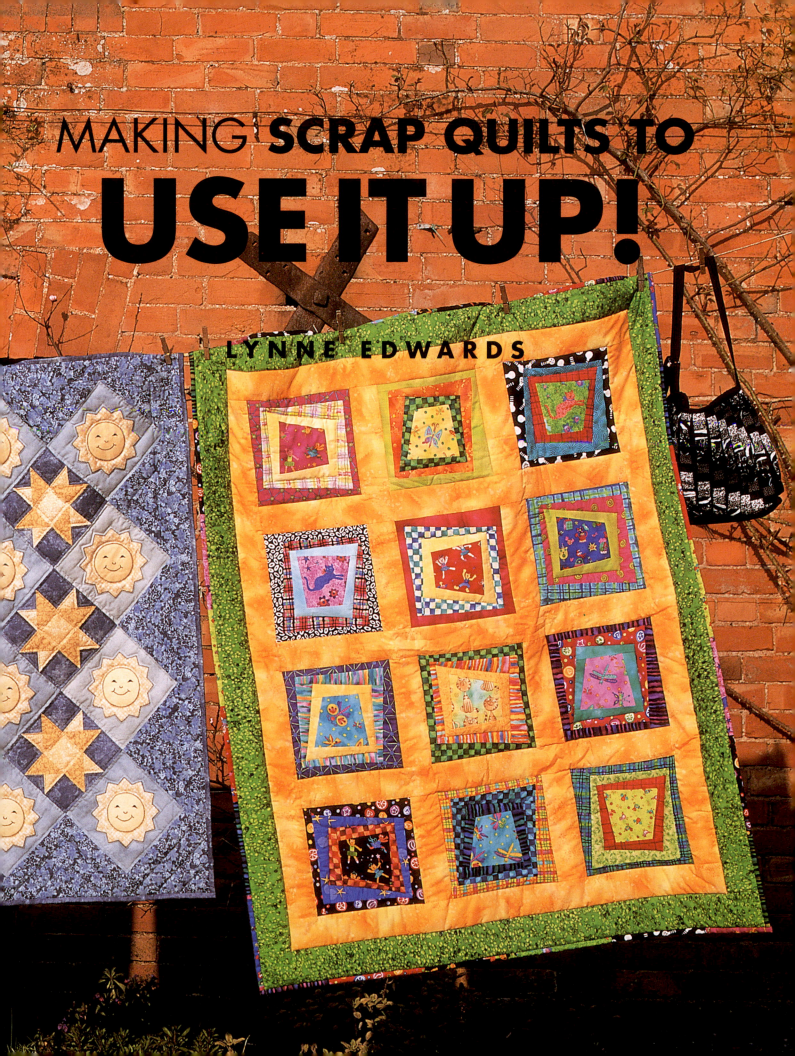

MAKING **SCRAP QUILTS TO** USE IT UP!

LYNNE EDWARDS

*To all my family and especially to my beloved sister-in-law Anne, who has been my
confidante and best friend for more than forty years.
To Della Chapman, whose friendship I value more than I can say.
Also of course to the Chelsworth quilters, who keep me on my toes at all times.
All I ask is a little respect. . .*

A DAVID & CHARLES BOOK
Copyright © David & Charles Limited 2003, 2006

David & Charles is an F+W Publications Inc. company
4700 East Galbraith Road
Cincinnati, OH 45236

First published in the UK in 2003
Reprinted 2004
First US paperback edition 2003
Reprinted 2004 (twice), 2006
First UK paperback edition 2006

Text and designs copyright © Lynne Edwards 2003, 2006

A catalogue record for this book is available from the
British Library.

ISBN-13: 978-0-7153-1411-1 hardback
ISBN-10: 0-7153-1411-4 hardback

ISBN-13: 978-0-7153-1412-8 paperback
ISBN-10: 0-7153-1412-2 paperback

Printed in China by SNP Leefung
for David & Charles
Brunel House   Newton Abbot   Devon

Photography by David Spaull and Kim Sayer

Visit our website at www.davidandcharles.co.uk

David & Charles books are available from all good bookshops;
alternatively you can contact our Orderline on 0870 9908222
or write to us at FREEPOST EX2 110, D&C Direct, Newton
Abbot, TQ12 4ZZ (no stamp required UK only); US customers
call 800-289-0963 and Canadian customers call 800-840-5220.

about the author

Lynne Edwards teaches and demonstrates a wide range of patchwork and quilting techniques, both hand and machine. She has written several textbooks that are considered to be definitive works.
In 1992 Lynne was awarded the Jewel Pearce Patterson Scholarship for International Quilt Teachers. This is in recognition of outstanding qualities as a teacher and included a trip to the Houston Quilt Market and Festival. The award led to invitations to teach as part of the Houston Faculty in 1993 and 1995 and at the Symposium of the Australasian Quilters' Guild in Brisbane in 1993. Since then international teaching trips have included venues in Europe, in Missouri, and the National Quilt Show in South Africa. In 2000 teaching commitments included Durban in South Africa and the National Canadian Festival, Canada 2000.
Her long association with the quilting movement both locally and nationally has involved Lynne in the organization of quilt shows from a local village hall to the Quilters' Guild National Exhibitions. She has served on selection committees and is an experienced judge of National Quilt Shows. She was Senior Judge at the South African National Quilt Show in 1998, her first experience of judging overseas. In 2000 Lynne was given honorary lifetime membership of the Quilters' Guild of the British Isles and in 2002 was awarded the Amy Emms Memorial Trophy for services to quilting.

Contents

Introduction

I have been making quilts and collecting fabric for many years. Some of my students have been coming to classes for fifteen years, so altogether there has been a lot of fabric piling up in this part of eastern England.

Only quilters understand the compulsion to stroke, sigh over and finally purchase yet more fabric. Jane Barff, one-time treasurer of the Quilters' Guild of the British Isles, gave me the perfect answer to all those non-quilters who ask 'Why are you buying fabric when you have so much already?' The answer she gave was 'Do stamp collectors use their stamps on letters?' We buy because we love the fabric, because it is an irresistible bargain, because we need a rich palette to dip into for our creative ideas. It never

seems to work to go out to a quilt shop to buy fabrics for a specific project so we buy a bit here, a bit there, for that as yet unspecified future project.

Inevitably some of that fabric we keep so long that we don't like it any more. Some has faded on the edges (haven't we all?), some is too lovely a design to cut up and some just intimidates because it was *so* expensive. I realized I had a problem when fellow-quilter Katharine Guerrier told me that I had more fabric than the shop in Bath. I had to accept that I had to start using it up. I needed the space to buy more fabric and I am certainly not leaving it to anyone. My long-term students feel the same, so for two years now I have been offering different designs,

techniques and projects that cover a wide range of ideas with the possibility of using up some of those stored treasures.

Scraps, of course, are included, but let's face it, quilters don't just have scraps, they have *yardage*. Most of the projects allow the flexibility to use lots of different fabrics and to substitute others when one runs out. There is a heady freedom in sewing two pieces together to make the last square needed for the quilt – isn't that what patchwork is all about?

Don't be afraid that the joy of purchasing fabric will be denied you. When students have returned with completed quilts they all seem to say the same thing, 'What really pleased me about this quilt is that I didn't buy any new

fabric for it. . .' pause. . . 'except of course. . .'

It is rare to complete a whole quilt without resorting to just one essential purchase for the sashing or for a border or cornerstones and so on, but at least the main ingredients will be from your own existing stash. Strange, then, that at the end of all your efforts the piles of fabric seem to be bigger than when you started. I think it must be the result of letting air get between all the layers as you choose so that when the quilt is finished there seems to be more fabric left than there was before.

Take heart! There are twenty different projects for you to work through, ranging from a pleated drawstring bag to full-size quilts. Start sorting that fabric right *now*.

Sort Out Your Fabric

Some of the designs in this book use teams of fabrics that have been arranged into lights, darks and mediums, like the two Split Nine-patch quilts (pages 47 and 51), or just lights and darks, like Phyll Howes-Bassett's Corner Log Cabin on page 22. Phyll's quilt is truly random – she has not considered colour grouping at all, just lights and darks, as has Jenny Lankester in her little Squares and Triangles quilt on page 57. Many of the quilts, however, have been through a certain amount of colour selecting before the mixing process has begun. This is understandable, as we choose the colours that please us most when we initially buy the fabric.

My collection has very few autumn shades in it – I go for blues, greys, mauves, subtle shades and no primary colours. The only reds that creep in are deep reds that look good with blacks and greys. Do not worry if your fabrics seem limited in their range of colours. Group the chosen fabrics together and see how they look as a team. Hopefully you will also be able to include a few that you now wonder why on earth you bought them. The more fabrics you use in the project, the easier it is to slip these oddballs in.

There are no fixed rules with fabric selection. You can grit your teeth and use *everything* in the real scrap tradition, or you can blend and design with your scraps to give a subtle and toning effect. Try one of the smaller projects to use up a group of fabrics that you bought as a pack and now wonder what to do with them. I stepped out of character a couple of years ago and bought a multi-pack of brilliant and brightly-patterned fabrics to make. . . something. . . sometime. They finally got used by Shirley Prescott to make the Crazy quillow on page 105.

If when sorting your fabrics you find some that you know you really hate and can never ever use, set them aside. Here is a thought: you do not have to use them. Ever. You can donate them to another quilter, you can take them to a school for the children to cut up. You can even put them in the fabric recycling bank. You will be able to stroke and enjoy the remaining goodies so much more easily without these villains. As you sort and group your fabrics you will discover all kinds of buried treasure that will inspire and excite you. Stroke them for a little while, and then use them up.

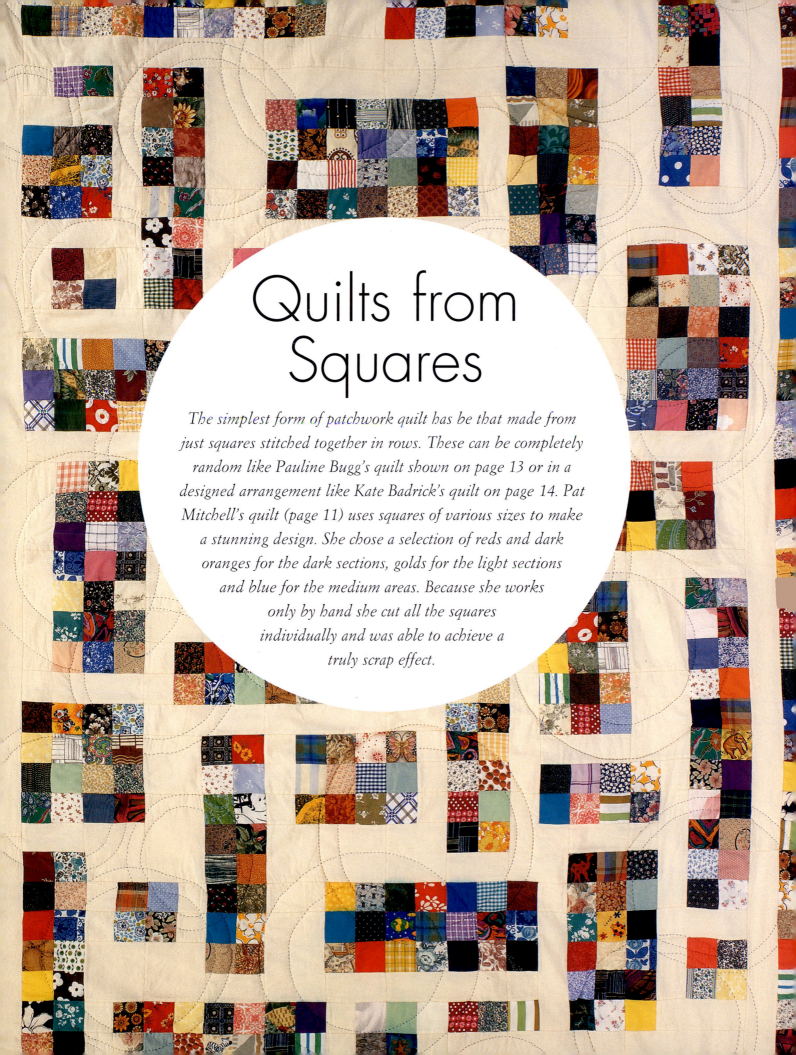

Quilts from Squares

The simplest form of patchwork quilt has be that made from just squares stitched together in rows. These can be completely random like Pauline Bugg's quilt shown on page 13 or in a designed arrangement like Kate Badrick's quilt on page 14. Pat Mitchell's quilt (page 11) uses squares of various sizes to make a stunning design. She chose a selection of reds and dark oranges for the dark sections, golds for the light sections and blue for the medium areas. Because she works only by hand she cut all the squares individually and was able to achieve a truly scrap effect.

All Square Quilt

This quilt uses squares of different sizes to produce an effective change of scale (Fig 1), with each of the three different blocks finishing as 4½in (11.4cm) squares. The nine-patch blocks in the centre form a dense area of small squares. These open out into the larger-scale squares of the four-patch blocks, which also fill the corners of the quilt. The large 4½in (11.4cm) squares add to the chequerboard effect and prevent the design from becoming too busy.

Finished size of blocks 4½in x 4½in (11.4cm x 11.4cm)

Finished size of quilt 86½in x 86½in (219.6cm x 219.6cm)

Fabric Requirements

You could use just three fabrics throughout but it will be much richer if you use quite a few. Two fabrics could be combined to make the nine-patch blocks and another two to make the four-patch blocks. Different fabrics could be used to make the large squares instead of one dark, one medium and one light. Begin by making the pieced blocks, laying them out and playing with the remaining fabric to see what looks best for the large squares. The border can be decided upon once the main quilt is pieced as it is always easier to judge what looks good at this stage.

2½yd (2.30m) of dark fabric for the dark squares of the design.

2¼yd (2m) of light fabric for the light squares.

3yd (2.70m) of medium fabric for the medium shade squares.

Borders: 1½yd (1.40m).

Backing fabric: 88in x 88in (223.5cm x 223.5cm).

Wadding: 88in x 88in (223.5cm x 223.5cm).

Binding: 24in (60.9cm) of 42in wide fabric.

Construction
Making the Nine-patch Blocks

Twenty-nine nine-patch blocks are needed for the quilt (Fig 2). They are constructed from rotary-cut strips for speed and accuracy.

Fig 1

1 Cut two dark strips and one light strip for band A, each 2in (5cm) wide and 41in (104cm) long (Fig 3). Cut three sets of these strips. They can be in shorter lengths provided the *total* length is at least 123in (313cm).

Cut two light strips and one dark strip for band B, each 2in (5cm) wide and 31in (79cm) long (Fig 3). Cut two sets of these strips. They can be in shorter lengths provided the *total* length is at least 62in (158cm).

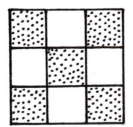

Fig 2

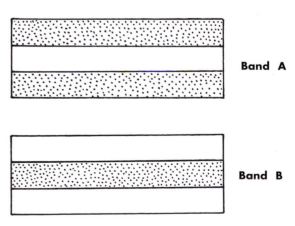

Band A

Band B

Fig 3

'My quilt is a continuation of my medieval interest. It conjures up the 1520 meeting on
"The Field of the Cloth of Gold", with the colours created by the tents and banners.
Another quilt in red, gold and blue and still fabric left over.' **Pat Mitchell**

2 Using a smaller stitch than for dressmaking (about two-thirds of the size) and a ¼in (6mm) seam, stitch together each band of strips. Alternate the direction of stitching the strips as this helps to keep the band flat and not rippled. Press each band from the front, ironing all the seams towards the darker fabric (Fig 4).

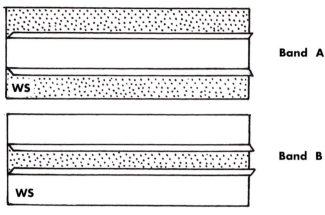

Fig 4

3 From band A cut fifty-eight pieces each 2in (5cm) wide (Fig 5). From band B cut twenty-nine pieces each 2in (5cm) wide (Fig 6).

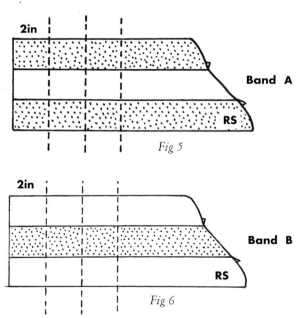

Fig 5

Fig 6

4 Take two pieces from band A and one piece from band B and arrange them on a flat surface as in Fig 7. Pin and stitch the three pieces together, matching seams carefully. Finally press the two vertical seams away

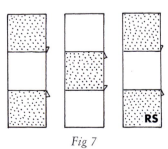

Fig 7

from the centre of the block as in Fig 8. Assemble the other twenty-nine nine-patch blocks in the same way. Time and thread can be saved if you stitch the blocks in a chain, one after the other, without taking them off the machine and breaking the thread after each block. Cut the thread between each block once they are completed.

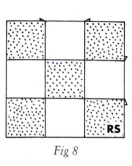

Fig 8

Making the Four-patch Blocks

For this quilt 108 four-patch blocks are needed (Fig 9). Sixty are used in the central area and forty-eight in the corners of the quilt.

Fig 9

5 For the centre area four-patch blocks, cut one dark strip and one light strip, each 2¾in (7cm) wide and 42in (106.5cm) long. Cut four sets of these strips. They can be in shorter lengths provided the *total* length is at least 168in (427cm).

6 Using the same smaller stitch length and the usual ¼in (6mm) seam, stitch together each set of two strips. Press the seams towards the darker fabric, ironing from the front (Fig 10).

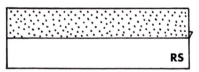

Fig 10

7 From the stitched bands cut 120 pieces each 2¾in (7cm) in width (Fig 11).

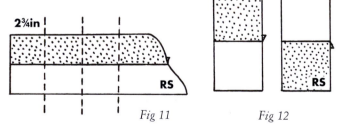

Fig 11   *Fig 12*

8 Take two cut pieces and arrange them in a four-patch as in Fig 12. Pin and stitch the pieces together, matching seams carefully. Finally press the seams to one side, ironing from the front (Fig 13). Assemble the other fifty-nine four-patch blocks in the same way, chain sewing the pairs of strips to save time and thread.

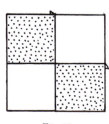

Fig 13

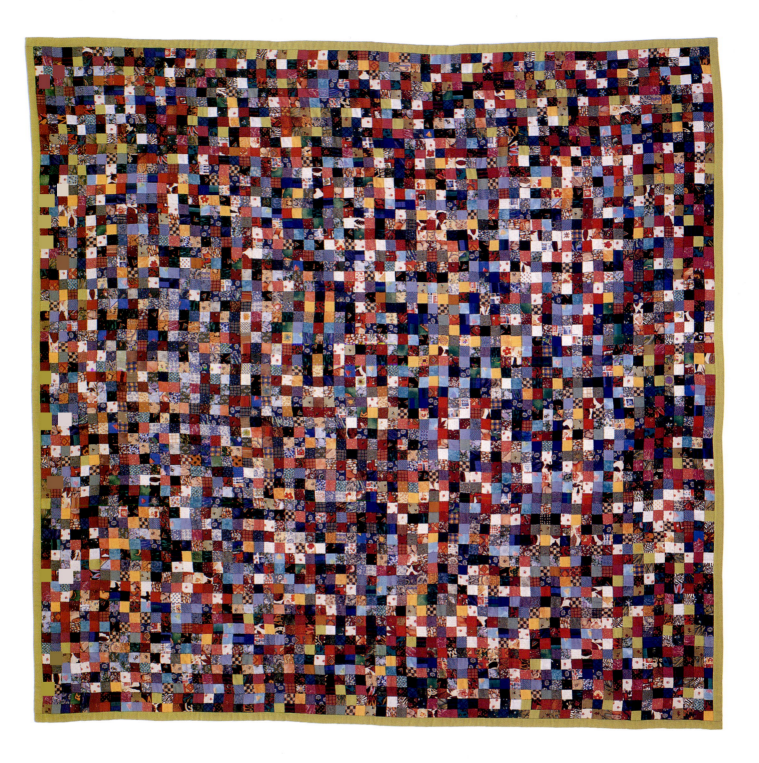

This quilt by Pauline Bugg is made entirely from scraps of unselected fabrics cut into squares and stitched together, each square 1½in (3.8cm) finished size. Although the arrangement of squares seems random, the central area has more light squares in it, while darker squares predominate towards the edges of the quilt. 'When I was introduced into the world of patchwork and all the beautiful fabrics I wanted them all, so I began collecting small pieces to satisfy my craving. After the initial excitement had died down I put together this scrap quilt – a reminder of how it all began.' **Pauline Bugg**

9 For the four-patch blocks used in the corners of the quilt cut one dark strip and one light strip, each 2¾in (7cm) wide and 34in (86.3cm) long. Cut three sets of these strips. They can be shorter lengths provided the *total* length is at least 102in (259cm).

10 Stitch and press the bands in the same way as the other four-patch blocks (Fig 10). From the stitched bands cut ninety-six pieces, each 2¾in (7cm) wide (Fig 11). Now assemble the forty-eight four-patch blocks from these pieces in the same way as before (Fig 12).

11 Cut the following one-square blocks, each 5in x 5in (12.7cm x 12.7cm): 40 squares of dark fabric; 32 squares of light fabric; 152 squares of medium fabric. You may have already planned which fabric or group of fabrics to use, or you can do it now by laying out the completed nine-patch and four-patch blocks in the quilt design shown in Fig 1 and trying out your possible one-square fabrics with these blocks in position.

12 Once you are happy with the arrangement of blocks pin and stitch the top row of nineteen blocks together, matching seams carefully. Take particular notice of the arrangement of the four-patch blocks – it is very easy to twist them into the wrong position without noticing. Press the row from the front, pressing the seams to one side.

13 Pin and stitch the second row together. Press the seams in the opposite direction to those in row 1. Continue to pin and stitch each row together, pressing the seams of each row in the opposite direction to the row above it. Place each stitched row back in position so that you can check the design. There are nineteen rows to be joined.

14 Join the rows together, matching seams carefully. Press seams to one side from the front. There is no border to this quilt but if you prefer to add one, see page 117.

Quilting

Pat's quilt was quilted by hand diagonally in both directions through all the blue squares in the design. For more ideas on quilting see page 122. The quilt was bound in the blue fabric (see Finishing a Quilt page 117).

This quilt by Kate Badrick uses squares of coloured fabrics grouped in blocks with interest created in the design by the placement of strips of cream fabric between the coloured areas.

'Several bags of scraps, fingers that needed to be occupied while watching television and a liking for doing patchwork over papers started this quilt. Initially it was to be entirely coloured squares but this looked overpowering, so irregular groups of squares were arranged on a calico background. The design was quilted in random circles of varying sizes.'

Kate Badrick

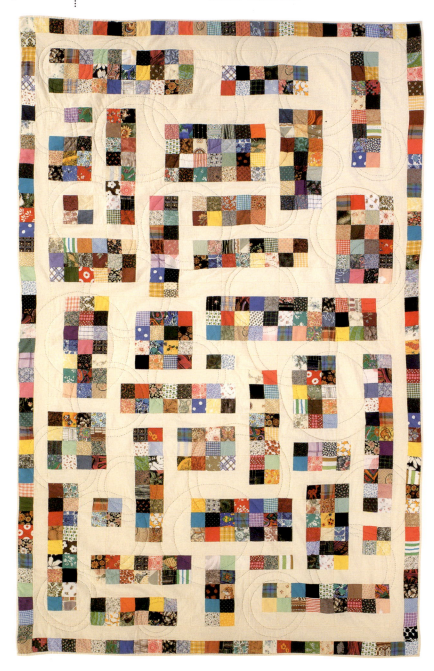

Quilts from Strips

Quilt designs built on strips are a marvellous way of using up some of that hoarded fabric. You may be able to cut across the fabric giving strips as long as 44in (112cm), but many will be far shorter. Strips cut down the fabric parallel to the woven selvage will be much firmer. It is almost impossible to avoid cutting both types of strips when using left-over fabrics, so use the more stretchy strips with care, trying not to pull them when stitching. It may help to spray-starch all the fabric before cutting into strips to keep the strips firmer.

Continuous Corner Log Cabin

Designs like Corner Log Cabin and Pineapple have a regular strip width but use many different fabrics in short lengths, so even small pieces can be cut into strips and used. This block begins in one corner with a square and is built out on two sides only with strips. The unusual method of continuous piecing means that the maker cannot consciously choose each collection of strips on each block – they just keep growing, each one finishing up with a different combination of fabrics.

Finished size of block 7½in x 7½in (19cm x 19cm)

Finished size of quilt As desired

Fabric Requirements

Like most Log Cabin designs the fabrics used need to be sorted into two clearly recognized teams. These might be different colours or sets of light and dark fabrics. My lap quilt, right, uses fourteen different fabrics in grey/blue/silvery tones for one set. If you can find fifteen to twenty fabrics for each colour team, the resulting multi-tonal scrap quilt will be really effective, although you could manage with only ten to twelve fabrics in each set. I cheated with the second set of fabrics for my quilt. I had a couple of yards of a multi-coloured 'dawn-sky' fabric with yellow, pink and blue and used it for all the strips in the second fabric set.

The amount of fabric needed will vary according to the size of quilt desired. A single bed will take about 6½yd (6m) of fabric in total using eighty blocks plus borders. A double quilt takes about 9½yd (9m) of fabric to make a hundred blocks plus borders. My lap quilt needed thirty-six blocks plus borders, about 3yd (2.75m) in total.

Cutting the Strips

Sort the fabric into two sets A and B, using as many different fabrics as you can. Cut just a few strips from each fabric to maintain the scrap effect. Put all the strips in Set A in one box or bag and the strips in Set B in another box or bag. When you need a strip do not carefully select one, just reach in, take one out and *use* it. The only time you should reject a strip is if it is the same as the one you have just used. Suggested width of strips – 2in (5cm).
Suggested length – any length more than 12in (30cm).

The technique will seem very strange as you begin it but once you get going, it's hard to stop! You do need to follow the instructions and the accompanying diagrams as you go along. I'm afraid the quilter's usual practice of 'When all else fails, read the instructions' only applies once you have made a few blocks. Set A and Set B fabric strips are shown in all diagrams as in Fig 1.

Set A   **Set B**

Fig 1

Construction

1 From a 2in (5cm) wide strip of fabric from Set A, cut one square 2in x 2in (5cm x 5cm). Place a strip of fabric from Set B on the sewing machine, right side *up* on the machine in the correct position for a ¼in (6mm) seam to be sewn. Lower the pressure foot and wind the needle down into the fabric. Now the pressure foot can be lifted and the square of fabric added without the first strip slipping out of position. Place the square from Set A right side *down* on the strip. Using a short stitch (about two-thirds normal sewing length) and a ¼in (6mm) seam, stitch the fabric square A on to the strip.

2 Remove the strip from the machine and carefully trim it to match square A. Finger-press the seam away from the corner square A (Fig 2).

3 Place the block right side *down* to the left of the sewing machine. Arrange it in the same position as in Fig 2. Now pick up a different strip from Set A and place it on the machine right side *up* ready to stitch. Wind the needle down into the fabric as before. Lift the pressure foot. Pick up the block and place it on to the strip without altering the position or turning it over, in the same arrange-

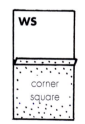

WS

corner square

Fig 2

In my Continuous Corner Log Cabin lap quilt I used fourteen different fabrics in grey/blue/silver
tones for one set, but just one multi-coloured fabric for the other,
resulting in this multi-tonal but muted scrap quilt

ment as in Fig 2 and with right side *down*. Stitch the block to the strip with a ¼in (6mm) seam.

4 Remove the strip from the machine and trim carefully to match the block. Finger-press the seam away from the original corner A square (Fig 3). *At the same time* cut a new square from the strip A that you've just been using (Fig 3).

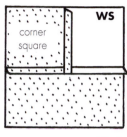

Fig 3

5 Place the block right side *down* to the left of the machine in the arrangement shown in Fig 3. Place the new cut square A on top of the block over the corner square, also right side *down*. This means you have two layers of fabric arranged by your machine.

6 Stack a different B strip on the machine right side *up* and wind the needle down into it. Lift the pressure foot. Pick up the top square A from the two layers and place it still with right side *down* on to strip B. Stitch the square to the strip and continue with a few more stitches, finishing with the needle *down* in the fabric.

7 Lift the pressure foot. Pick up the remaining block and move it across on to the B strip that is on the machine. Keep the block in the same position and right side *down* as in Fig 3. Stitch the block to the B strip as in Fig 4. You now have two blocks stitched on one strip of B fabric.

8 Remove the strip from the machine. Trim the B strip carefully to match the new corner square A and the block. Finger-press the seams away from the corner square (Fig 5).

9 Place the larger block right side *down* by the machine in the position shown in Fig 5. Stack the smaller block on top of it, also with right side *down*, as in Fig 5, with the corner

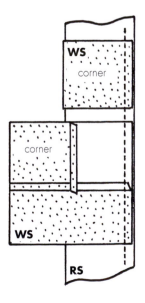

Fig 4

squares of both blocks lying on top of each other. The blocks are now in two layers.

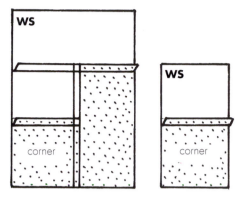

Fig 5

10 Place a different A strip on the machine right side *up* and sink the needle into it. Lift the pressure foot. Pick up the top block from the two layers and place it on the A strip right side *down* and in the same arrangement as in Fig 5. Stitch the block to the strip and continue with a few more stitches, finishing with the needle *down* in the fabric.

11 Lift the pressure foot. Pick up the larger block and move it across on to the A strip that is on the machine. Keep the block in the same position and right side *down* as in Fig 5. Stitch the block to the A strip as in Fig 6.

12 Remove the strip from the machine. Trim the A strip carefully to match the two blocks. Finger-press the seams away from the corner squares. *At the same time* cut a new square from the A strip that you have just been using (Fig 7).

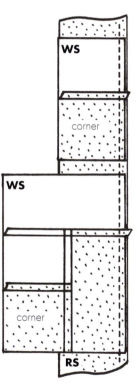

Fig 6

Tip

Each time an A strip is used, a new corner square is cut from it to begin the next new block.

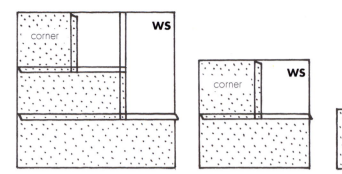

Fig 7

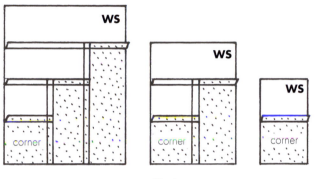

Fig 8

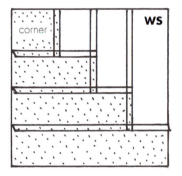

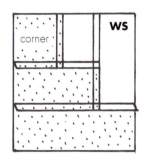

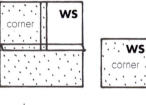

Fig 9

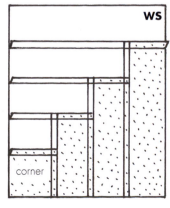

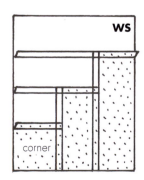

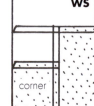

Fig 10

13 Place the largest block right side *down* by the machine in the arrangement in Fig 7. Place the next size block on to it, right side *down* in the same arrangement with the corner square of each block directly on top of each other. Finally, lay the new cut A square right side *down* over the corner squares. There are now three layers of fabric by the machine.

14 Place a different B strip on the machine right side *up*. Place each block in turn right side *down* on the strip in the same arrangement as they were layered (Fig 7) and stitch them on to the strip.

Tip

When stitching blocks to a B strip, the corner square should always appear in the top left-hand corner. When stitching blocks to an A strip, the last B strip should lie horizontally along the top of the block.

15 Remove the B strip from the machine. Trim the strip carefully to match the three blocks (Fig 8). Finger-press the strips away from the corner blocks.

16 Arrange the blocks right side *down* by the machine, largest first. Layer the other blocks on top in the same positions as Fig 8, finishing with the smallest on top.

17 Place a different A strip on the machine, right side *up*. Place each block in turn right side *down* on the A strip, smallest first, and stitch them on to the strip.

18 Remove the A strip from the machine and trim to match the three blocks. Finger-press the scams away from the corner square. *At the same time* cut a new corner square from the A strip that you've just been using (Fig 9).

19 You now have four blocks to work with. Arrange the largest block by the machine right side *down* as in Fig 9. Place the other three blocks on to it also right sides *down* in the same arrangement with the smallest block (the single corner square) on top. Position the corner squares all on top of each other in each layer.

20 Place a different B strip on the machine, right side *up*. Place each block right side *down* in turn on to the strip and stitch. Trim the strip to match the four blocks (Fig 10).

Quilts from Strips

Shirley Prescott used carefully chosen fabrics to give a Monet feeling to her quilt, although the positioning of each fabric in each block was still random and beyond her control.
'My daughter gave me an antique plate with the colours she wanted used in this quilt for the old sofa in her farmhouse kitchen, hence the muted blues and greens with a dash of pink. The total effect made us call it "à la Monet".' **Shirley Prescott**

If the strip of fabric isn't long enough for all four blocks, take a new strip from the same set and continue to sew the blocks on to that.

21 Arrange the largest block – this will be its final strip – by the side of the machine right side *down* as in Fig 10. Arrange the other three blocks on to it right sides *down* with the smallest on the top, ready for stitching.

22 Place a different A strip on the machine right side up. Place each block right side *down* in turn on to the strip and stitch. Trim the strip to match the four blocks. Finger-press the seams away from the corner squares. The largest block is now complete (Fig 11), so set it aside. *At the same time* cut a new square from the A strip that you have just been using. This begins the new fourth block so you now have a collection as in Fig 9.

From now on just follow the sequence outlined in steps 19–22 above. Each time a block is completed, a new square of A fabric is cut, so there are always four blocks being processed, although they are all at different stages. This helps to give the scrap effect as no two blocks are the same.

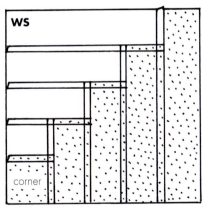

Fig 11

Assembling the Quilt

Press each block from the front. You will doubtless find that the blocks are not all exactly the same size. If any need to be trimmed to bring them to the right measurement, trim on the two seamed sides (Fig 12). Lay the blocks out to find a design that pleases you. Any classic Log Cabin arrangement like Barn Raising will be suitable. If your blocks will not stretch to make a large enough quilt, consider making a centre area of the blocks, framing it with strips and then moving into a different colour scheme of blocks to extend the quilt.

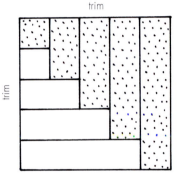

Fig 12

Adding Borders

If you are using limited left-overs, adding borders may be a problem. I added two rows of joined pieces from my Set A strips to make a frame around the blocks, then a border from all I had left of my 'dawn sky' fabric. For ideas on borders see Bordering a Quilt page 117.

Quilting

I gave my own small quilt to Jenny Spencer to quilt with her long arm machine. She quilted a very attractive overall swirly design that really enhanced the quilt. Phyll did not quilt the main part of her quilt but tied it at regular intervals with a machine-quilted border. For more ideas on quilting see page 122. The final edges were bound with several different fabrics joined together (see Finishing a Quilt page 117).

Phyll Howes-Bassett's quilt shows just how effective unplanned scraps can be. She just took all her left-overs and sorted them into two piles, one light and one dark. Any fabric that hovered uncertainly between the two was mercilessly excluded.

'When I started this quilt I tried to group the scraps into pleasing combinations, which didn't work at all! Finally I had to be brave and just put my hand in each bag of dark or light strips and use whatever I pulled out – a real scrap-bag effort.' **Phyll Howes-Bassett**

Jenny Lyons selected a group of strong greens and blues for her scrap pineapple quilt (see project which follows) and used them with a team of mixed creams and beiges to create a real contrast.

'To make this quilt I cut hundreds of fabric strips and divided them into light and dark piles. I then sewed pineapples for three days, picking random strips within the light and dark pattern – pure therapy!' **Jenny Lyons**

Sashed Pineapple Quilt

The Pineapple design is perfect for using up groups of scrap fabrics. It is a close relative of Log Cabin, the main difference being that the strips in the Pineapple are not just stitched in a square around a centre but also at 45° to the centre, making a more complex eight-sided design. Traditionally, the design is drawn on to a foundation fabric and the strips stitched to this. Specialist Pineapple rulers now make the task easier (see page 126), although there is less control over the general accuracy and joining many blocks often means some fudging. The addition of sashing strips between blocks reduces the need for corners to match up exactly and adds interest.

Finished size of Pineapple block (before sashing)
9½in x 9½in (24cm x 24cm)

Finished size of quilt 61in x 95½in (155.8cm x 242.4cm)

Fabric Requirements

Sue FitzGerald used four different green and four different pink fabrics in her blocks with a plain pink and green for each four-patch centre. These were balanced with an equal amount of cream calico fabric as background which was also used for the sashing strips between each block. For your quilt choose two distinct and different teams of fabrics that you feel look good together, plus a third fabric for background. This does not have to be a neutral shade, as in Sue's quilt. It could be a strong dark colour or even a mixture of very similar fabrics used together to enhance the scrap effect of the quilt.

Scrap fabrics: 1¾yd (1.60m) each of two teams of fabrics, as many different fabrics in each team as possible for the Pineapple blocks, cornerstones and binding.

Background and sashing: 4yd (3.65m) of a third fabric.

Working with a Foundation

To ensure accuracy of piecing a Pineapple block I suggest using a foundation piecing technique. The foundation, or base on which the design is drawn and to which the fabrics are stitched, can be one that is removed once the block is completed, like paper or a tear-away foundation, or one that is left permanently in place like calico. It helps to be able to see through the foundation, so tracing paper or freezer paper are both excellent, or a woven tear-away foundation could be used which can be purchased from fabric shops.

Preparing for Sewing

Stitching along a drawn line on a foundation is easier if an open-front foot is used on the machine so you can see both needle and line as you stitch. Use a larger size 90/14 needle as this makes larger holes in the foundation, making it easier to remove. For the same reason, reduce the stitch length to about 18–20 stitches to 1in (2.5cm). Do a test run on a measured inch on some fabric and count the stitches to find the correct setting for your machine.

Construction

1 Cut a square of foundation 10½in x 10½in (26.5cm x 26.5cm) and fold it lightly into quarters (Fig 1).

Fig 1

2 Trace the design shown in Fig 2 page 29 on to a quarter of the foundation, matching the dotted lines in the diagram with the folds in the foundation (Fig 3). Number the lines as in Fig 2. Turn the foundation and position a second quarter over the design in Fig 2, matching the dotted lines and folds as before. Trace the design on to the foundation and add the numbers. Repeat this in the remaining two sections of the foundation to complete the full Pineapple design.

3 Cut strips for the Pineapple blocks all 1½in (3.7cm) wide. A strip length of about 40in (101.5cm) is needed for each block in each colour, plus about 80in (203cm) for the background strips. These do not have to be in long lengths – several shorter strips that together add up to the required length will be fine.

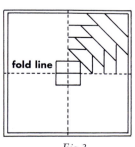

fold line

Fig 3

The various fabrics in Sue FitzGerald's quilt have been used in the blocks and arranged in a symmetrical design that is really pleasing to the eye. Jenny Lyons' scrap pineapple quilt (page 23) does not include sashing and gives a denser effect with strips of many fabrics and a rich use of colours.

'I used all the pink and green scraps left over from my first sampler quilt for this project. I really enjoyed working with the Pineapple design, especially with the sashing, which made assembling and matching the blocks so much easier.' **Sue FitzGerald**

Making the Four-patch Centres

For the centre of each block Sue FitzGerald used the same two fabrics throughout which were made into four-patch units and then placed on the foundation. It is easier to make all the four-patches for the quilt at the same time.

4 Cut strips of each of the two chosen fabrics each 1½in (3.7cm) wide and 86in (218.3cm) long. This length can be made from several shorter strips, as long as the total length is at least 86in (218.3cm). Place the strips together, right sides facing and stitch them together with a ¼in (6mm) seam, using a smaller stitch than usual (Fig 4). Now open the strips out and press the seams towards the darker fabric, working from the front (Fig 5).

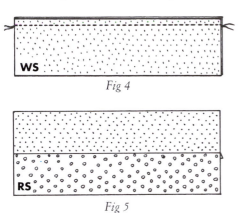

Fig 4

Fig 5

5 Cut the strips vertically into 1½in (3.7cm) wide pieces (Fig 6). Take two pieces and turn the second piece through 180° (Fig 7). Place the two pieces right sides facing, matching the centre seam then pin and stitch the two pieces together. Press the seam to one side, ironing from the front (Fig 8).

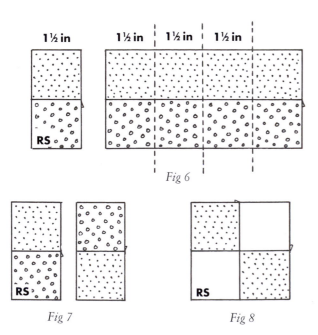

Fig 6

Fig 7   *Fig 8*

6 Continue to pin and stitch each four-patch until twenty-eight units have been made. Time and thread can be saved if the blocks are stitched in a chain, one after the other, without taking them off the machine and only cutting the thread between each block once they are completed.

7 Place one four-patch unit right side *up* on the unmarked side of the foundation (this is the front) over the drawn centre four-patch on the design. Hold it in position and turn the foundation over. Adjust the position of the four-patch so that the seamlines are lying exactly underneath the drawn four-patch on the foundation and the centres are matched. It should overlap the drawn four-patch centre by ¼in (6mm) on all sides. If you cannot see too well through the foundation hold it up against the light on the sewing machine. Pin the four-patch in position, as in Fig 9.

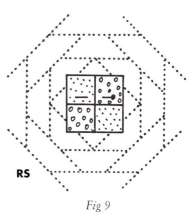

Fig 9

8 To make Round 1, from a strip of background fabric cut four pieces each 2½in (6.3cm) long. Place one piece on the pinned square, right sides facing, with the edges matching (Fig 10). Pin in position, keeping the pin well away from the seam allowance where the stitching will be. Turn the foundation over to the drawn side (the back of the block). The numbers show the order of stitching. Stitch along the drawn line marked 1 through both thicknesses of fabric, extending two or three stitches beyond the beginning and end of the drawn line (Fig 11).

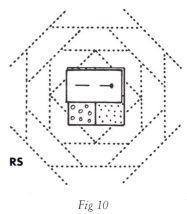

Fig 10

9 Turn to the right side and trim the seam allowance down to a scant ¼in (6mm) by eye with sharp scissors. Flip the strip over on to the

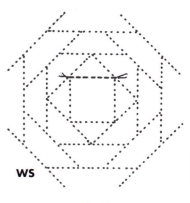

Fig 11

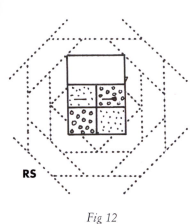

Fig 12

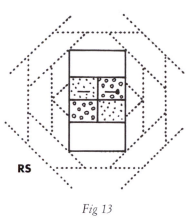

Fig 13

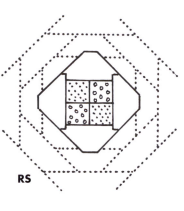

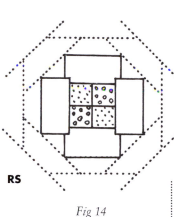

Fig 14

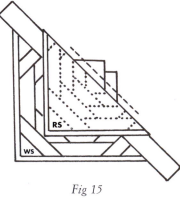

Fig 15

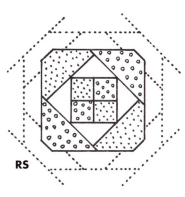

Fig 16

Fig 17

foundation, finger-press the seam and press with an iron from the front (Fig 12).

10 Repeat this process with a second piece of fabric on the opposite side of the centre square. Press it over on to the foundation as before, as in Fig 13.

11 In the same way pin and stitch the remaining two pieces to the other sides of the centre square. Press over on to the foundation (Fig 14).

12 Cut two pieces from a strip in the first colour (A) and two pieces from a strip in the second colour (B) each 3½in (8.9cm) long. These will make Round 2 of the design. It is not easy to position these strips in the correct place on the front of the block because the line is masked by the fabric already stitched to the foundation. It helps to trim the stitched lengths down at this stage. Turn the foundation to the marked side and place a thin ruler along the next stitching line (marked 2 on the foundation). Pull the foundation back along this line against the edge of the ruler. Don't worry if the foundation pulls away from the stitches at the end of the seams. Trim the fabric by eye to a scant ¼in (6mm) beyond the folded edge of the foundation (Fig 15). Do this on all four sides on each line marked 2 on the foundation (Fig 16).

13 Position one cut strip of fabric A on one of the trimmed sides of the block with right sides facing, lining up the edges. Pin in position and turn the foundation over to the marked side. Stitch along the drawn line marked 2 through both layers of fabric, sewing two or three stitches beyond the drawn line at the start and finish. Turn to the right side and flip the fabric over on to the foundation. Press into position with an iron. Repeat this with the second cut strip of fabric A on the opposite side. Then repeat the process with the two cut strips of fabric B on the other two sides of the block, pressing each strip out on to the foundation as they are stitched.

14 Trim the excess fabric from the block by turning the foundation to the drawn side and placing a ruler along each line marked 3. Pull the foundation back against the edge of the ruler and trim the fabric to a scant ¼in (6mm) beyond the folded edge of the foundation (Fig 17).

15 From a strip of the background fabric cut four pieces each 3¾in (9.5cm) long. Pin and stitch them to each side of the block, stitching along the drawn lines marked 3 on the foundation. This makes Round 3 of the design. Flip each piece over and press on to the foundation. Use a ruler placed on the lines marked 4 to trim the fabric down as before. You will find that as the block progresses gaps appear between the pieces of fabric along each edge and you may not need to trim the fabric back to be able to position the next round of strips accurately. Just do whatever makes it easiest for you.

16 The next round of strips (Round 4) uses two pieces of fabric A and two of fabric B, each 4½in (11.4cm) long. Stitch fabric A to the two sides that already have this fabric stitched on them and fabric B to the two sides that already have fabric B stitched to them (Fig 18 overleaf).

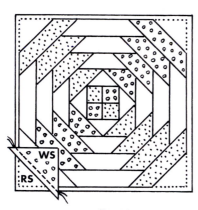

Fig 18

17 Continue to build out the block, stitching four strips each time along the marked lines. The length of strip used each time is as follows:

Round 5: four strips of background fabric each 4½in (11.4cm) long.

Round 6: two strips of fabric A and two strips of fabric B, each 5¼in (13.3cm) long.

Round 7: four strips of background fabric each 5¼in (13.3cm) long.

Round 8: two strips of fabric A and two strips of fabric B, each 6¼in (15.9cm) long.

18 For the final corners cut one square from fabric A and one square from fabric B each 4in x 4in (10cm x 10cm). These are slightly larger than necessary but it is better to have a little extra to trim down to the final size. Cut each square diagonally to make the four corners. With right sides facing, pin the longest edge of each triangle to the corners of the block – fabric A corners on the fabric A strips, and fabric B corners on the fabric B strips. Stitch along the drawn lines marked 9 on the foundation (Fig 19). Press the corners back on to the foundation.

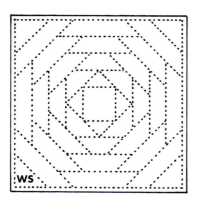

Fig 19

19 Trim the block and foundation to exactly ¼in (6mm) beyond the outer drawn line. This makes a block 10½in x 10½in (26.5cm x 26.5cm).

20 Make a total of twenty-eight Pineapple blocks in this way, drawing out each block on the foundation and stitching it in the same way. Use a different combination of fabrics from the two collections of A and B in each block.

21 Arrange the twenty-eight blocks in horizontal rows of four blocks, seven rows altogether. Leave a space between each block for the sashing strips. Move the blocks around until you are satisfied with the balance of the quilt.

Adding Sashing Strips

The sashing strips are all cut from the background fabric, with cornerstones in the two collections of scrap fabrics.

1 From the chosen background fabric cut sixty-seven strips, each 2½in x 10½in (6.3cm x 26.5cm). Pin and stitch a sashing strip between the blocks of the top row and also at either end (Fig 20). Repeat this for all seven horizontal rows of blocks. Press the seams towards the sashing, ironing from the front.

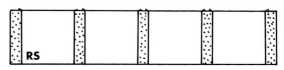

Fig 20

2 Arrange the seven rows of blocks and place the remaining cut sashing strips between them and at the top and bottom of the quilt so that you can decide which scrap fabrics will look best in each of the cornerstones as in Fig 21.

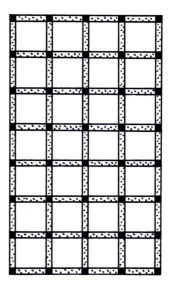

Fig 21

3 From the chosen cornerstone fabrics cut a total of forty squares each 2½in x 2½in (6.3cm x 6.3cm). Pin and stitch the top row of cornerstones and sashing strips together (Fig 22). Press seams towards the sashing strips. Place this joined strip at the top of the quilt.

RS · · · · · · ·

Fig 22

4 Continue to stitch together the remaining seven strips of cornerstones and sashing. Place them in position so that you can check the balance of fabrics in the quilt.

5 Pin and stitch the horizontal rows of sashing strips to the blocks, matching seams carefully. Press the long seams towards the sashing, ironing from the front. Once the sashings are stitched in place remove the foundation.

Adding Borders

Sue's quilt has a narrow frame of scrap fabric cut 1½in (3.7cm). If you don't have enough left of any of the fabrics used in the quilt, choose something else that will frame the quilt effectively. Sue added a border of background fabric cut 6in (15.1cm) wide and bound the quilt with one of her scrap fabrics. A pieced binding from all the left-overs would be equally good (see Bordering a Quilt page 117 and Binding a Quilt page 123).

Quilting

Sue quilted a series of curving lines across her quilt to break up the angular effect of the Pineapple design. She echoed this in the wide border with a ribbon-like curved plait. For more ideas and instructions on finishing and quilting see pages 117 and 122.

Fig 2

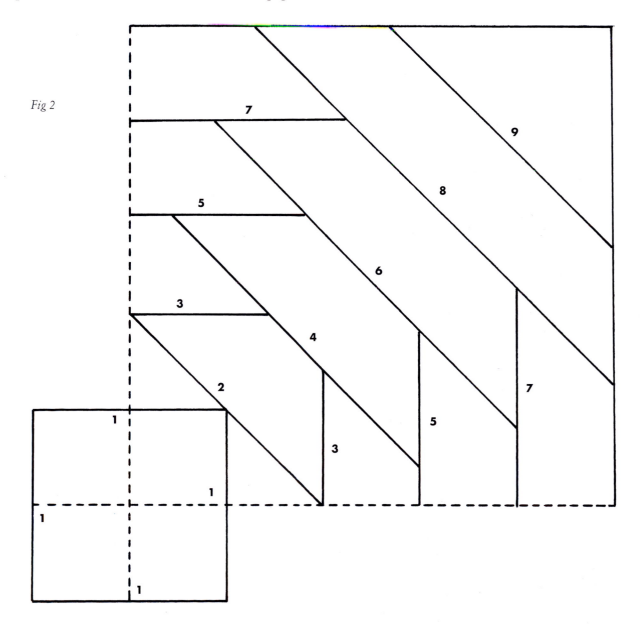

Magic Lantern Quilts

This effective quilt is made from the lantern block. It looks really difficult, full of spiky corners that need precision cutting and stitching, but it is actually quick and easy to make. The block is made using one of those stitch, cut, and stitch again techniques that is more suitable for machine stitching. Two quilts are described here. The bed quilt (right) made by the Winchcombe team uses the larger block. My own smaller lap quilt (shown on page 35) uses smaller templates and has a more intricate border. Full instructions are provided for both, as the change of scale in the block is important for the overall effectiveness of the quilt design.

Magic Lantern Bed Quilt

Finished size of lantern design (two blocks combined)
12in x 9in (30cm x 22.8cm)

Finished size of quilt 64in x 88in (163cm x 223cm)

Fabric Requirements

This quilt can have a different fabric for each lantern, about forty fabrics, but is just as effective with a limited number used several times in the quilt. Each lantern is cut from a strip of fabric 8in x 14½in (20cm x 36.8cm). The design looks best with one background fabric used throughout, although you might get away with several very similar fabrics combined for the backgrounds.
Background fabric: 3½yd (3.20m).
Border and binding: ¾yd (68.5cm).

Construction

1 From a selection of fabrics chosen for the lanterns cut strips 8in (20cm) wide. A strip 14½in (36.8cm) long will give two triangles, enough for one complete lantern. For the background areas in the design cut strips 8in (20cm) wide. Two strips each 5½in (14cm) long will give four triangles, enough for all the background in a complete lantern block. Use long strips of background fabric if you have them to make cutting more economical. Make card templates by drawing shapes A and B from Fig 1 (page 32), cutting them out and sticking them on to card, or use template plastic. If you have a 60° ruler you can probably use it instead of the templates (see rulers page 126). This is a machined technique so seam allowances are included in each template.

2 Place Template A (the 60° triangle) on a cut strip of lantern fabric 8in x 14½in (20cm x 36.8cm). Several strips of different fabrics can be layered together and cut at the same time if wished. Line up the flattened corner of the triangle with the top of the cut strip as shown in Fig 2. The bottom of the strip should be level with the edge of the template. Draw along both sides of the template with a sharp pencil (Fig 3). Left-handers should work from the right-hand edge of the strip.

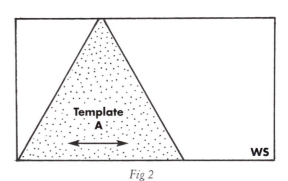

Fig 2

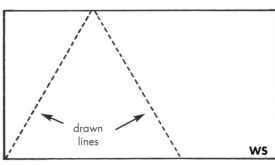

drawn lines

WS

Fig 3

*'We decided to use the 60° triangle to make a scrap quilt for charity. Pooling our most colour-
ful remnants we spent several happy afternoons producing the lantern quilt illustrated.'*
Gwen Bryson and the Winchcombe Quilters

3 Turn the template around and place it so that the right-hand drawn line on the fabric exactly lines up with one edge of the template. Draw along the other edge of the template (Fig 4 page 33).

4 Remove the template and use a ruler and rotary cutter to cut along the drawn lines. This will give two 60° triangles which will make one lantern. Cut thirty-nine sets of these triangles for the quilt.

5 Take two strips of background fabric 8in (20cm) wide and in whatever length you were able to cut. Place the two strips right sides together *exactly* on top of each other. Straighten the left-hand edges of the strips. Position the 30° template B on the strip with the straight long side matching the left-hand edge of the fabric as in Fig 5. The flattened corner of the template should line up with the top edge of the strip. The short side of the template should be level with the bottom edge of the strip. Left-handers should work from the right-hand end of the strip. Draw along the slanted edge of the template. Also draw along the angled corner at the top of the template (Fig 6).

6 Turn the template around and place it so that the drawn slanted line on the fabric exactly lines up with the slanted side of the template. Draw along the straight side of

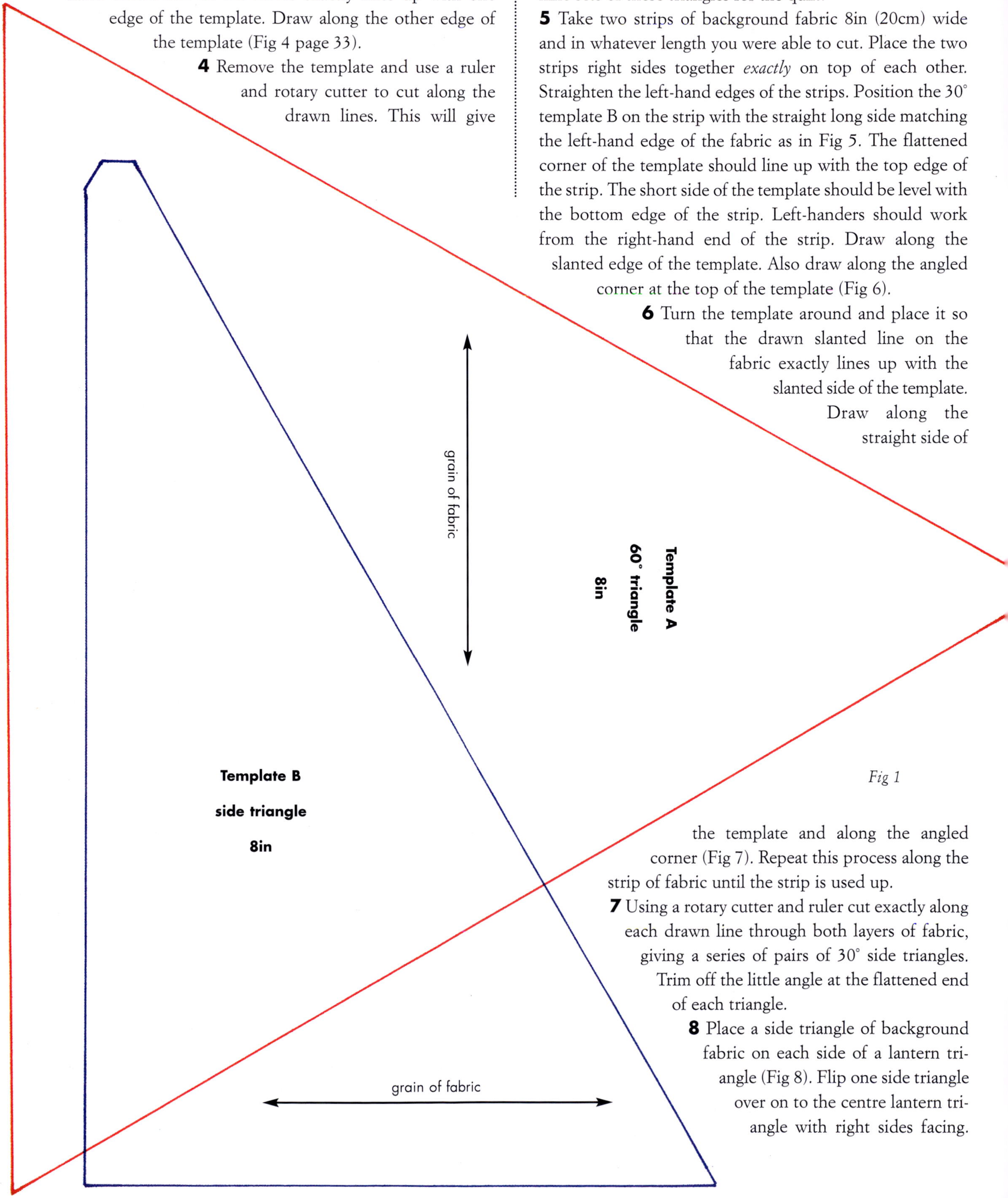

grain of fabric

Template A

60° triangle

8in

Template B

side triangle

8in

Fig 1

grain of fabric

the template and along the angled corner (Fig 7). Repeat this process along the strip of fabric until the strip is used up.

7 Using a rotary cutter and ruler cut exactly along each drawn line through both layers of fabric, giving a series of pairs of 30° side triangles. Trim off the little angle at the flattened end of each triangle.

8 Place a side triangle of background fabric on each side of a lantern triangle (Fig 8). Flip one side triangle over on to the centre lantern triangle with right sides facing.

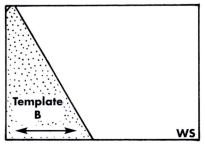

Fig 4

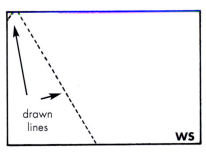

Fig 5

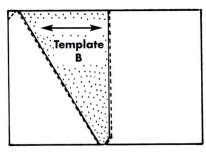

Fig 6

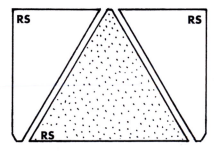

Fig 7

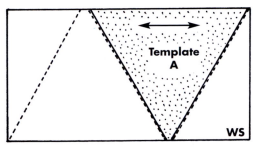

Fig 8

Line up the long diagonal edges, matching the trimmed corner of the background triangle with a sharp corner of the lantern fabric (Fig 9). Pin and stitch a ¼in (6mm) seam (Fig 10). Press the side triangle out from the lantern triangle, ironing from the front.

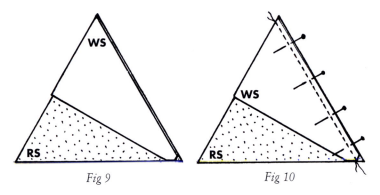

Fig 9   *Fig 10*

9 In the same way pin and stitch the opposite side triangle to the lantern triangle (Fig 11). Press this side triangle out from the lantern triangle, ironing from the front (Fig 12). Trim off the little extending triangles from the top and side edges of the block.

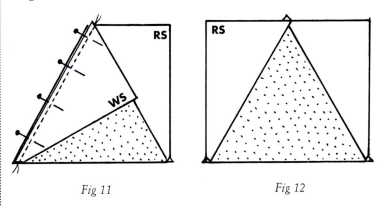

Fig 11   *Fig 12*

10 The block should now measure 8in from top to bottom (*not* from side to side). Cut the block horizontally into four strips each *exactly* 2in (5cm) wide (Fig 13). Turn each strip round through 180°, keeping in the same order (Fig 14).

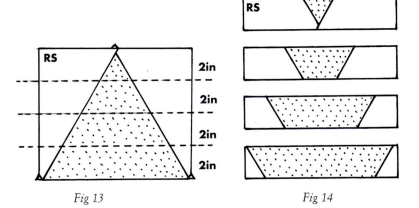

Fig 13   *Fig 14*

11 Stitch the four strips together with a ¼in (6mm) seam, matching both ends carefully (Fig 15). This block is then half of the lantern design. Press the seams away from the longest strip of lantern, ironing from the front.

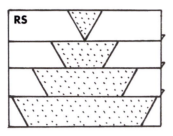

Fig 15

12 Repeat the process from steps 8–11 using a triangle of the same lantern fabric and two background side triangles as before.

13 Stitch the two halves of the lantern design together using a ¼in (6mm) seam and matching corners carefully (Fig 16). Press the centre joining seam open to balance the block. Continue to make the lantern blocks until you have thirty-six complete lanterns and six separate half lanterns.

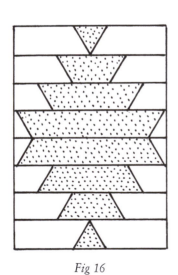

Fig 16

Assembling the Quilt

First stitch the lantern blocks into six vertical rows as Fig 17. Note that rows 1, 3 and 5 have a half lantern placed at the *bottom* end of each row. Rows 2, 4 and 6 have a half lantern placed at the *top* end of each row. This makes an interesting arrangement of lanterns on the quilt.

Pin and stitch rows 1 and 2 together with a ¼in (6mm)

seam as usual, matching seams carefully. Continue to add each row until all the six rows are joined. Press the long vertical seams open to give a smooth look to the quilt.

Adding Borders

A border of background fabric using 3in (7.5cm) cut strips allows the lantern blocks to float within the final purple border. This was also cut 3in (7.5cm) wide and used once more to bind the quilt (see Bordering a Quilt page 117).

Quilting

Gwen, Joan and Betty quilted the Winchcombe quilt with hand quilting ¼in (6mm) away from each lantern, plus machine quilting in diamonds on the background frame and purple border. (For more ideas on quilting and instructions for binding see pages 122 and 123.)

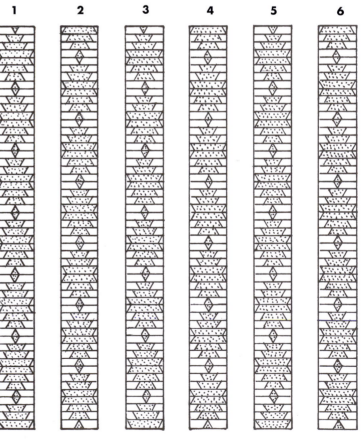

Fig 17

Magic Lantern Lap Quilt

My lap quilt (below) uses a smaller size lantern and has a border of 60° triangles, mainly because I had no pieces of fabric left that were long enough to make a framing border. I also gave the quilt more of a scrap look by joining two different half lanterns together and spreading them randomly over the quilt.

Finished size of lantern design (two blocks combined)
8in (20cm) tall x 6⅝in (16.8cm) wide

Finished size of quilt 47in x 50in (119.3cm x 127cm)

Fabric Requirements

I used about twenty different suede-effect hand-dyed fabrics that I had been collecting in bundles. They had been designated 'too good to use' so at last I took the plunge and cut them up – not easy! The blue background is from the fabric department of a large department store, an indigo chambray sold for summer dresses which I love and have had to replace in my store of fabrics as I know I will want to use it again.

Each lantern is cut from a strip of fabric 6in x 11in (15.2cm x 27.9cm). Eighteen complete lantern blocks and four half lantern blocks are needed for the design.

Background fabric: 2yd (1.83m) including border and binding.

Borders: each coloured border that frames the design can be squeezed out of a ¼yd (22.8cm) of fabric.

Construction

1 From a selection of fabrics chosen for the lanterns cut strips 6in (15.2cm) wide. A strip 11in (27.9cm) long will give two triangles, enough to make two half lanterns. These can both be joined with different half lanterns to vary the look of each block. For the background areas in the design cut strips also 6in (15.2cm) wide. Two strips each 4⅜in (11cm) long will give four triangles, enough for all the background in a complete lantern block (see block photo page 35). Use long strips of background fabric if you have them as this makes the cutting more economical.

2 Make card templates by tracing the two shapes AA and BB from Fig 1a (page 37), cutting them out and sticking them on to card, or use template plastic. If you have a 60° ruler you can probably use it instead of the templates (see rulers page 126). This is a machined technique, so seam allowances are included in each template.

3 Place template AA (the 60° triangle) on a cut strip of lantern fabric 6in x 11in (15.2cm x 27.9cm). Several strips can be layered together and cut at the same time if wished.

4 Now follow the instructions for drawing around templates, cutting and stitching the pieces detailed in steps 2–9 of the instructions for the Magic Lantern bed quilt (pages 30–33). Remember, *your* strips are 6in (15.2cm) wide *not* 8in (20cm), otherwise there is no difference.

5 The block should now measure 6in (15.2cm) from top to bottom, *not* from side to side. Cut the block horizontally into four strips each *exactly* 1½in (3.7cm) wide (Fig 13). Now turn each strip round through 180°, keeping them in the same order (Fig 14).

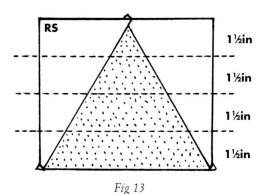

1½in
1½in
1½in
1½in

Fig 13

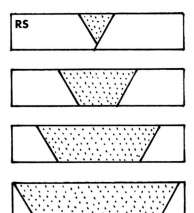

Fig 14

6 Stitch the four strips together with a ¼in (6mm) seam, matching both ends carefully (Fig 15). This block is now half of the lantern design. Press the seams away from the longest strip of lantern, ironing from the front.

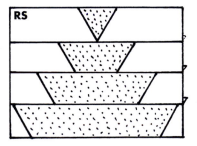

Fig 15

Fig 1a

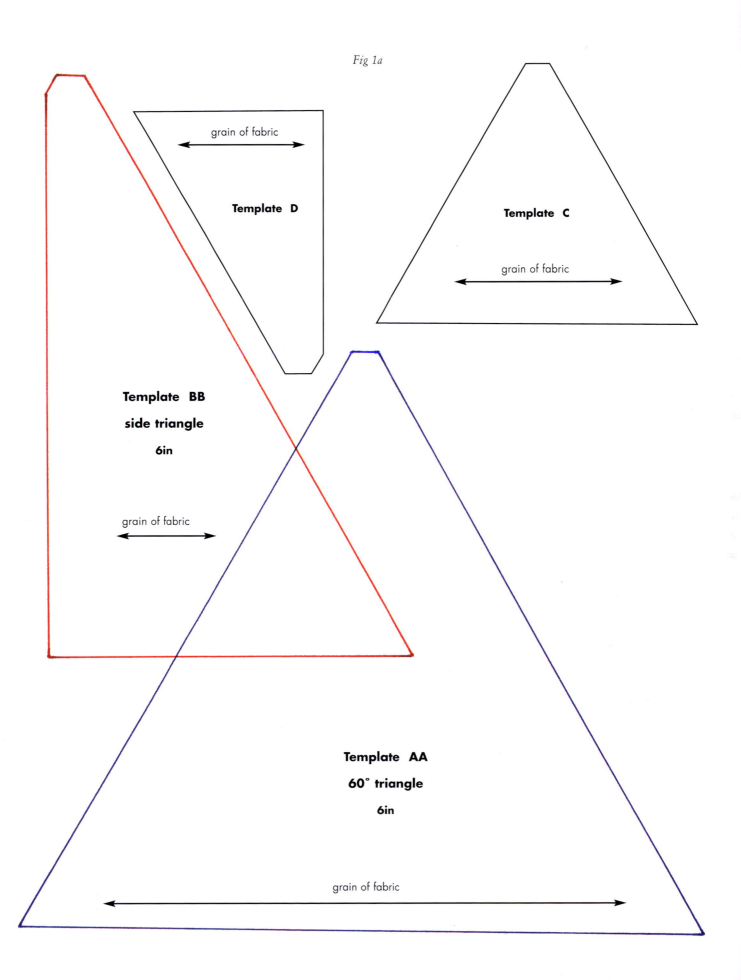

grain of fabric

Template D

Template C

grain of fabric

Template BB

side triangle

6in

grain of fabric

Template AA

60° triangle

6in

grain of fabric

7 Make forty half lantern blocks, then arrange thirty-six of them into pairs to make eighteen complete lanterns, mixing the fabrics well to give a balanced scrap effect. Stitch together the two halves of each lantern, matching corners carefully (Fig 16). Leave the last four half lanterns separate.

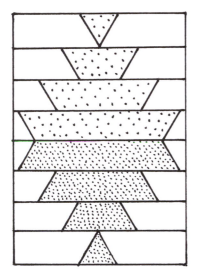

Fig 16

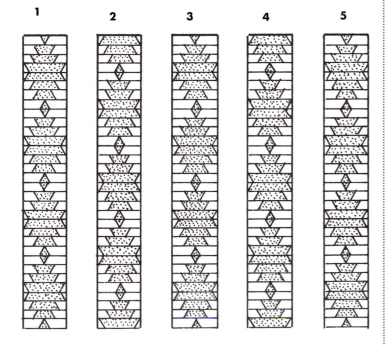

Fig 17

Assembling the Quilt

First stitch the lantern blocks into five vertical rows as in Fig 17. Note that rows 2 and 4 have a half lantern placed at

either end of the row. This makes an interesting arrangement of lanterns on the quilt. Pin and stitch rows 1 and 2 together with a ¼in (6mm) seam as usual, matching seams carefully. Continue to add each row until all five are joined. Press the long vertical seams open to give a smooth look to the quilt.

Adding Borders

When making a pieced border it is easier to construct the border strips first and then add framing strips to the quilt to bring it to a measurement that will fit the borders (see Adding Borders page 117).

1 To make the 60° triangle border make card templates from shapes C and D in Fig 1a (page 37).

2 From all the left-over lantern fabrics cut strips 2¾in (7cm) wide. A strip 9in (22.8cm) long will give four triangles, one for each pieced border strip on the quilt. From the background fabric cut strips also 2¾in (7cm) wide. Longer strips can be used and trimmed to match each strip of lantern fabric as it is used. Sixty-two triangles are needed from assorted lantern fabrics and fifty-eight from the background fabric, plus eight smaller 30° triangles and four squares 2¾in x 2¾in (7cm x 7cm) all from the background fabric.

3 Place a strip of background fabric and a strip of lantern fabric right sides together *exactly* on top of each other. Use template C to draw and cut pairs of triangles in the same way as when making the lantern triangles.

4 Lay the triangles in a row, alternating a lantern triangle with a background triangle as Fig 18. Check that the grain of fabric is always running along the outer edges of the design. Pin and stitch together twenty-nine triangles starting and ending with a lantern fabric (fifteen from lantern fabrics and fourteen from background). Repeat this to make two border strips for the top and bottom of the quilt.

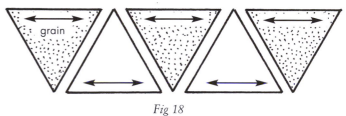

Fig 18

5 Pin and stitch together thirty-one triangles starting and ending with a lantern fabric (sixteen from lantern fabrics and fifteen from background). Repeat this to make the two side borders strips.

6 Take two strips of background fabric 2¾in (7cm) wide

and 6in (15cm) long. Place the two strips right sides together *exactly* on top of each other. Using template D, draw and cut four pairs of 30° triangles in the same way as when making the side triangles for the lantern block. These triangles are used at either end of each pieced border strip to straighten it (Fig 19).

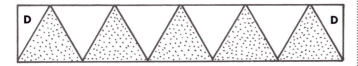

Fig 19

7 Compare the pressed pieced border strips with the sides of the quilt. Ideally they should measure 5in–6in (12.7cm–15cm) more than the quilt. Add one or two frames around the quilt to bring it up to fit the border strips exactly. I needed 2½in (6.3cm) all around my quilt to make it fit my border so I first added a frame, cut width 2in (5cm), finished width 1½in (3.7cm) and then another cut width 1½in (3.7cm), finished width 1in (2.4cm). If there is a problem getting the borders to fit, either trim the frame down a little or stretch out the triangular border with a steam iron.

8 Stitch the two side border strips to the quilt. Press seams outwards, ironing from the front (Fig 20).

Fig 20

9 Stitch a 2¾in (7cm) square of background fabric to either end of the top and bottom border strips. Press the seams in towards the border, ironing from the front (Fig 21).

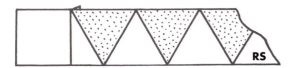

Fig 21

10 Pin and stitch the top and bottom border strips to the quilt, matching seams carefully. Press the seams outwards from the quilt, ironing from the front.

11 Add another frame of background fabric around the quilt – I used 2in (5cm) cut strips – to allow the design to float in the background fabric. Bind the quilt in the same fabric after quilting.

Quilting

I machine quilted around each lantern and once again about ½in (12mm) away, using the side of my walking foot as a guide. I repeated this on the border triangles and finally hand quilted large diamonds within each lantern. For more advice on finishing and quilting see pages 117 and 122.

Strip Snowball Quilt

The Snowball block has been made for many years and is composed of a square of fabric converted into an octagon by cutting off the four corners. In this quilt design the squares have been made from assorted strips of fabrics and the corners replaced with triangles in contrasting colours. Paddy Courtauld's quilt (right) is made from a collection of her husband's old shirts and even the tails of some still-used favourites! She stitched both red and blue corners to each block and added shirt buttons in addition to hand quilting the design. Janet Covell used the same design, but with homespun flannel fabrics, for her son's quilt, shown on page 44.

Finished size of Snowball block 7½in x 7½in (19cm x 19cm)

Finished size of quilt 63in x 100in (160cm x 254cm)

Fabric Requirements

For a single bed quilt twelve rows of blocks with seven blocks in each row are needed – a total of eighty-four blocks.

Blocks: about 6yd (5.5m) of assorted fabrics.

Corners: ½yd (45.7cm) of each of two contrast fabrics.

Borders: ¼yd (21.5cm) for the inner red frame and 1yd (91.4cm) for the outer wide border.

Binding: 21in (53.2cm) of one fabric or a mixture of fabrics already used in the blocks.

Construction

1 From the chosen selection of fabrics cut strips, some 1¾in (4.3cm) wide and some 2in (5cm) wide. Try to have roughly equal numbers of strips in each width. Cut each strip into 8¼in (21.5cm) lengths.

2 Take six strips in assorted widths and fabrics and lay them out side by side to check the effect of the arrangement. Stitch the strips together using a ¼in (6mm) seam and a smaller stitch. Press the seams of the stitched block all to one side, ironing from the front.

3 Trim the block to an *exact* 8in (20cm) square (Fig 1). Make as many of these 8in (20cm) stripped squares as you need for your project. Eighty-four are needed for this single bed design but if you want a different size quilt you can calculate how many blocks you'll need by remembering that a finished block is 7½in x 7½in (19cm x 19cm).

Adding the Corners

4 Each block needs two corners in one contrast fabric and two in the other contrast fabric (Fig 2). There is a painless

way of adding these corner triangles to the block that is easy and very accurate, if slightly wasteful of fabric. For each corner triangle cut a 2in x 2in (5cm x 5cm) square of contrast fabric. For the single bed quilt cut 132 squares 2in x 2in (5cm x 5cm) from each of the two corner fabrics.

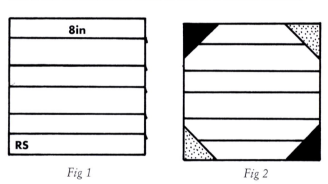

Fig 1   *Fig 2*

5 Place one square of corner fabric on to a corner of the stripped block right sides together, matching edges carefully (Fig 3) and pin it in position.

6 Stitch across the pinned square diagonally from corner to corner (Fig 4). To mark the line to be stitched draw a line on the wrong side of the fabric square with a marking pencil. Alternatively use masking tape, as described in the Tip overleaf.

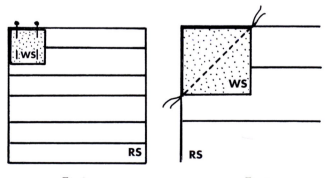

Fig 3   *Fig 4*

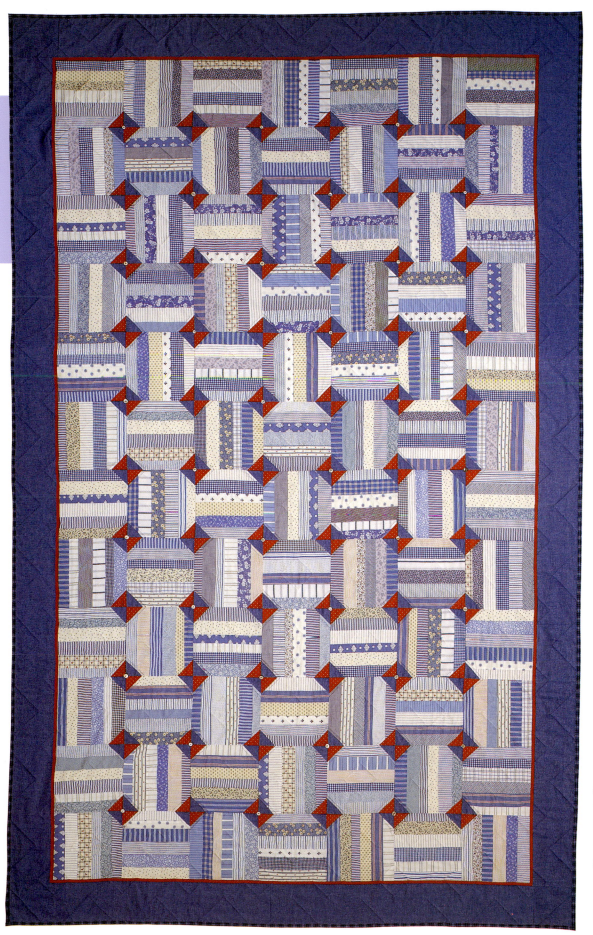

'This quilt was quick and easy to make and it was fun searching the house for fabrics and buttons. Not only were old shirts included but also a few pairs of discarded boxer shorts.'
Paddy Courtauld

Tip

To sew diagonally across a square of fabric without marking a guideline, stick a strip of masking tape on to the plate of the sewing machine with one edge level with the machine needle (Fig 5). Place the corner of the fabric to be stitched under the needle and position the opposite corner of the fabric exactly on top of the edge of the masking tape (Fig 6). Keep the bottom corner positioned on the edge of the masking tape at all times as you stitch the fabric.

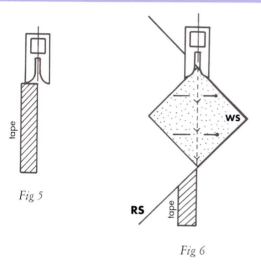

Fig 5

Fig 6

7 Trim the excess fabric ¼in (6mm) beyond the stitching line (Fig 7). The trimmed corners could be used later in a miniature quilt. . . possibly. . . Press back the triangle of fabric to make the corner of the square block, pressing the seam out towards the corner (Fig 8).

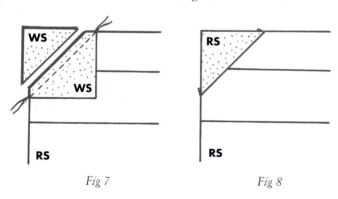

Fig 7

Fig 8

8 Add the other three corners to the block in the same way, using one fabric for two opposite corners and the second fabric for the other two corners (Fig 9).

9 For the design in Paddy's quilt shown on page 41 add four corners to twenty-five blocks as in Fig 9. Add four corners to twenty-five more blocks as in Fig 10. The corners are in the same arrangement of colours but the strips of

Fig 9

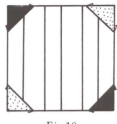

Fig 10

fabric have been turned from horizontal to vertical for the second set of twenty-five blocks. These fifty blocks form the centre of the quilt (Fig 11).

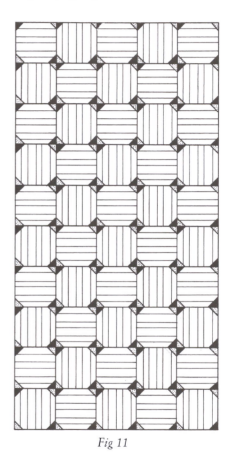

Fig 11

10 For the edging blocks add two corners to only fifteen blocks as Fig 12, then add two corners to fifteen more blocks as Fig 13. Once again the corners have stayed in the same arrangement but the strips in the blocks have been turned.

Fig 12

Fig 13

11 Finally, add one corner only to the remaining four blocks to make the corners of the quilt (Fig 14).

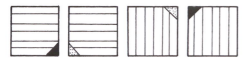

Fig 14

Assembling the Quilt

12 Arrange the centre fifty blocks as shown in Fig 11. Pin and stitch the top row of five blocks together with the usual ¼in (6mm) seams. Press the seams to one side, ironing from the front.

13 Pin and stitch the second row of five blocks together. Press the seams in the opposite direction to those of row 1, ironing from the front. Continue to pin and stitch each row, pressing seams in alternate directions to help lock them.

14 Join the rows together, matching seams carefully. Press seams to one side from the front. Arrange the five blocks for the top row as shown in Fig 15. Pin and stitch the row together. Press the seams in the opposite direction to row 1 on the main quilt.

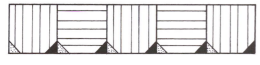

Fig 15

15 Join the top row to the quilt, matching seams carefully. Press the seam in the same direction as the other horizontal seams on the quilt.

16 Arrange the five blocks for the bottom row as shown in Fig 16. Pin and stitch the row together. Press the seams in the opposite direction to the bottom row on the main quilt.

Fig 16

17 Join the bottom row to the quilt, matching the seams carefully. Press the seam in the same direction as the other horizontal seams on the quilt.

18 Arrange the two side rows of blocks as in Fig 17. Pin and stitch both rows together. Press seams in the opposite direction to those on the main quilt.

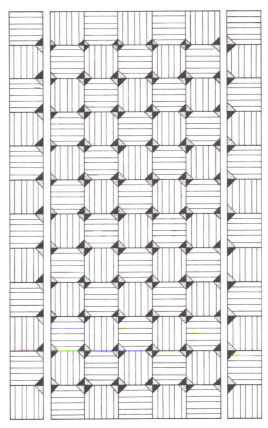

Fig 17

19 Join the two side rows to the main quilt, matching seams carefully. Press the seams outwards from the main quilt, ironing from the front.

Adding Borders

Paddy's quilt has a narrow frame of red cut 1in (2.4cm) wide followed by a wider border of blue cut 4½in (11.3cm) wide. It was bound in one of the shirting fabrics used in the quilt (see Bordering a Quilt page 117).

Quilting

The quilt was quilted as shown in Fig 18. The border design is shown at the side of the blocks. In addition, buttons were stitched firmly through all layers at each alternate junction of four blocks. For binding edges see page 123.

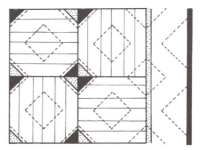

Fig 18

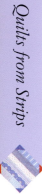

Quilts from Strips

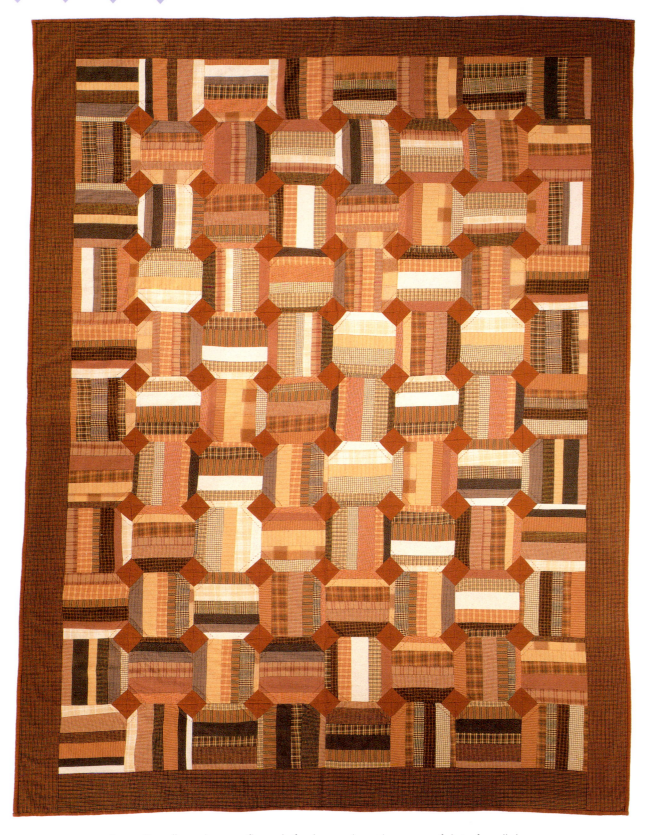

Janet Covell used warm flannels for her quilt, with just one fabric for all the corners to keep the quilt simpler. She tied through the layers rather than quilt the design (see page 122).
'I made this quilt for my son Richard before he moved to Switzerland – it is a little bit of home that he took with him.' **Janet Covell**

*My Split Nine-patch quilt for Judith O'Hagan,
based on an English herb garden.*

Starry Night Scrap Quilt

Jane Marshall made this quilt of stars (right) for her daughter Georgia using all her collection of yellows plus a wide variety of blues and purples. Each 6in (15.2cm) block (left) is a simple star cut from one yellow fabric on a background of blue or purple. Every block has a different combination of one yellow and one blue/purple fabric and the scrap effect is accentuated by sashing and cornerstones in a mixture of all the different blues and purples. It really is a stunning little quilt.

Finished size of block 6in x 6in (15.2cm x 15.2cm)

Finished size of quilt 46½in x 61½in (118cm x 156.2cm)

Fabric Requirements

1½yd (137cm) of assorted yellow fabrics for stars.

2yd (182.8cm) of assorted blue/purple fabrics for background, sashing, cornerstones and binding.

Construction

1 For each block cut the following: from a yellow fabric cut one square 3½in x 3½in (8.8cm x 8.8cm) and four squares 2⅜in x 2⅜in (6cm x 6cm); from a blue fabric cut one square 4¼in x 4¼in (10.8cm x 10.8cm) and four squares 2in x 2in (5cm x 5cm).

2 Each block is made from a centre square, four small corner squares and four pieced Flying Geese units (Fig 1).

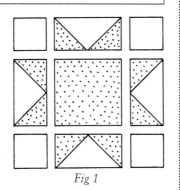

Fig 1

Making the Flying Geese Units

3 Take the 4¼in (10.8cm) square of blue background fabric. Draw both diagonals on the *right* side of the fabric with a sharp marking pencil (Fig 2).

4 Draw one diagonal on the *wrong* side of each of the four 2⅜in (6cm) squares of yellow fabric (Fig 3).

Fig 2

Fig 3

5 With right sides together pin two of the small yellow squares on to the blue square, lining up the drawn diagonal lines. The two corners of the smaller square will overlap in the centre (Fig 4). Trim these corners off, following the drawn line on the large square so that the two smaller squares meet but do not overlap (Fig 5).

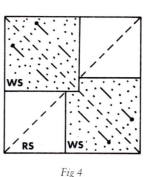

Fig 4

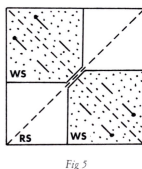

Fig 5

6 On the yellow squares machine a seam on each side of the drawn diagonal lines exactly ¼in (6mm) from the line (Fig 6). If you do not have a ¼in foot for your machine to stitch this seam accurately, try one of the following:

❖ If your machine has the facility, move the needle until the distance between it and the side of the foot is exactly ¼in (6mm);

❖ Using a different colour of marking pencil to avoid confusion, draw a line ¼in (6mm) away from the diagonal line on both sides.

7 Cut along the drawn diagonal line between the

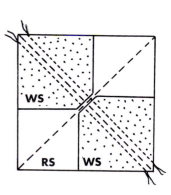

Fig 6

'This quilt was designed for my daughter, who asked me to make her a blue quilt with gold stars on it. I wanted to do a simple design that could be made up quickly but have fun with graduating fabrics and colours. We chose the fabrics from my stash together, then I made the individual blocks. Originally it was going to be a simple "lighter in the middle and dark around the edge" layout, but up on my design wall it evolved into this less rigid shading.'

Jane Marshall

two stitched lines (Fig 7).

8 Take one section and finger-press the small triangular pieces away from the main triangle (Fig 8).

9 With right sides together, pin a small yellow square on to the main blue triangle, matching the drawn diagonals (Fig 9). Machine a seam on either side of the diagonal line on the small square exactly ¼in (6mm) from the line (Fig 10).

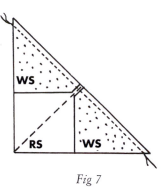

Fig 7

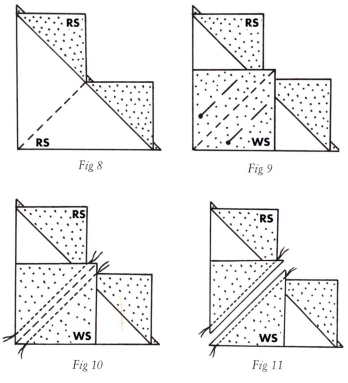

Fig 8

Fig 9

Fig 10

Fig 11

10 Cut along the drawn line between the two stitched lines (Fig 11).

11 Repeat steps 8–10 with the remaining pieced section and the small yellow square. Press each piece from the front with the seams lying towards the smaller triangles. You will now have made four identical Flying Geese (Fig 12). Trim the over-hanging corners of fabric level with the main block before continuing (Fig 13).

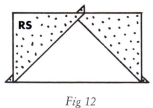

Fig 12

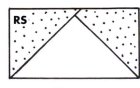

Fig 13

Assembling the Star Block

12 Arrange the Star block as in Fig 1 (page 52). Pin and stitch the top row together. Press seams towards the end squares, ironing from the front (Fig 14).

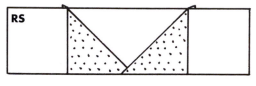

Fig 14

13 Pin and stitch together the middle row. When pinning a Flying Geese unit to the centre square, pin as shown in Fig 15 with the Flying Geese uppermost so that when you stitch you sew through the crossed seams in the centre. If you stitch right through this cross of stitches you will not cut off the point of the large triangle (Fig 16) – after all, who wants Flying Geese with bent beaks? Press seams towards the centre square, ironing from the front.

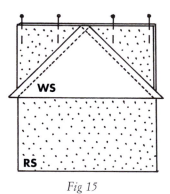

Fig 15

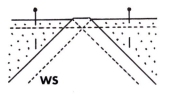

Fig 16

14 Stitch the third row together, pressing the seams towards the end squares: this way the seams will lock together when the three rows are joined to make the Star block.

15 Stitch the three rows together, matching seams carefully. Again, stitch with the Flying Geese units uppermost on the machine to make sure you do not cut off the points. Press the seams towards the centre, ironing from the front.

Tip
Each Star block should measure 6½in x 6½in (16.5cm x 16.5cm) at this stage. Check the measurement of this first block. If this is not exactly as it should be, adjust the seam allowances when making the second block until you get the right sizing. You can do some stretching out with a steam iron, but it is a good idea to sort out your seam allowance at the start rather than after you have made all forty-eight blocks!

Adding Sashing Strips

The sashing strips and cornerstones are cut from as many different blue/purple fabrics as possible.

1 From these assorted fabrics cut sixty-three strips each 2in x 6½in (5cm x 16.5cm). Also cut out sixty-three squares for the cornerstones each 2in x 2in (5cm x 5cm).

2 Lay out the blocks and arrange the sashing strips and cornerstones between them so that the colours and fabrics are distributed in an arrangement that pleases you. There should be six Star blocks in

each horizontal row and eight rows of blocks. There should also be a row of sashing around the edge of the quilt to form a border (Fig 17).

3 Pin and stitch a sashing strip between the blocks of the top row and also at either end (Fig 18). Repeat this for all eight horizontal rows of blocks. Press the seams towards the sashing, ironing from the front.

4 Pin and stitch the top row of cornerstones and sashing strips together (Fig 19). Press seams towards sashing strips. Place this joined strip at the top of the quilt.

5 Continue to stitch together the remaining eight strips of cornerstones and sashing. Place them in position so that you can check the balance of fabrics.

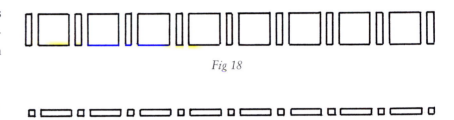

Fig 18

Fig 19

6 Pin and stitch the horizontal rows of sashing strips to the Star blocks, matching seams carefully. Press the long seams towards the sashing, ironing from the front.

Quilting

Jane's quilt is quilted entirely by machine with gold-coloured thread to outline the stars and a variegated blue/purple thread for the meandering vermicelli-type quilting on the background fabrics. For more ideas on quilting see page 122.

Binding the Quilt

There are no extra borders to this quilt. The binding is made from joined strips of dark blue and purple fabrics which blend in with the final rows of sashing around the edges of the quilt (See Finishing a Quilt page 117.)

Fig 17

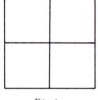

Quilts from Squares & Triangles

Squares and Triangles Quilt

This little quilt of Jenny Lankester's (right) combines a four-patch block with a square with knocked-off corners. She used nothing but left-over scraps and when she ran out of the plain cream fabric used in the block with knocked-off corners she just filled in with more four-patches.

Finished size of blocks 4in x 4in (10cm x 10cm)

Finished size of quilt 53in x 37in (134.5cm x 93.9cm)

Fabric Requirements

304 squares of left-over fabrics, as many different fabrics as possible, each 2½in x 2½in (6.3cm x 6.3cm).
40 squares of cream fabric each 4½in x 4½in (11.3cm x 11.3 cm).
Border: ½yd (45.6cm) fabric.
Binding: assorted scraps joined together.

Construction

Making the Four-patch Blocks

Fifty-six four-patch blocks are needed for this quilt. Arrange four squares of fabric, each cut 2½in x 2½in (6.3cm x 6.3cm) together as in Fig 1a. Stitch the squares into pairs. Press the seams from the front to one side, ironing the seam of the top pair of squares the opposite way to that of the bottom pair (Fig 2). Stitch the top pair to the bottom pair, matching seams carefully. Press the seam to one side.

Fig 1a   *Fig 1b*

Fig 2

Making the Knocked-off-corners Blocks

1 Forty knocked-off-corners blocks are needed for the quilt (Fig 1b). Cut forty squares of the main fabric, each 4½in x 4½in (11.3cm x 11.3cm).

2 Place a 2½in (6.3cm) square of fabric on to the top left-hand corner of the large square, matching edges carefully

and pining in position (Fig 3). In the same way pin a different 2½in (6.3cm) square on to the *opposite* corner of the large square.

3 Stitch across the pinned squares diagonally from corner to corner (Fig 4). To mark the line to be stitched either draw a line on the wrong side of the fabric square with a sharp marking pencil or use the alternate method described in the Tip on page 42.

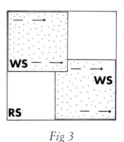 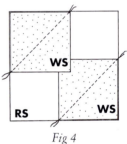

Fig 3   *Fig 4*

4 Trim excess fabric ¼in (6mm) beyond the stitching line (Fig 5). Press back the triangles to make the corners of the square block, pressing seams out towards the corner (Fig 6). Make all forty knocked-off-corners blocks in the same way.

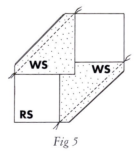 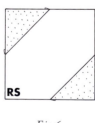

Fig 5   *Fig 6*

5 Arrange the two sets of blocks as shown in Jenny's quilt, right. There are eight blocks in each horizontal row and twelve rows of blocks to make the quilt.

6 Stitch the blocks together in horizontal rows, pressing the seams in alternate directions to help lock the seams. Now join the rows together, matching seams carefully and pressing seams to one side from the front.

Adding Borders

Jenny bordered the quilt with strips cut 3in (7.5cm) wide. Left-over fabrics were joined together for the binding. The quilt is tied at regular intervals, not quilted (see Bordering a Quilt, page 122). For more ideas on finishing see page 117.

'I have never made a scrap quilt before this one. Being a bit of a haphazard person myself and prone to going off at a tangent, the news that I could just throw everything in a bag and pick out at random appealed to me immediately.' **Jenny Lankester**

Snowball Nine-Patch Quilt

This quilt by Collie Parker (right) alternates a Snowball block with a nine-patch block. It is a real scrap quilt, using as many fabrics as possible with just one calming fabric used as the main shape in the centre of each Snowball block. To give some order to the arrangement it helps to limit the fabrics to two in each nine-patch block. Collie also used one fabric throughout for the corners on each Snowball. Alternatively, make these corners from different fabrics for a random effect. If you make some nine-patch blocks first you can then judge what will look best for the Snowball corners with your collection of fabrics. Joan Reeve's version of the design on page 65 uses a larger 9in (22.8cm) square block size and a limited number of fabrics.

Finished size of smaller blocks (nine-patch and Snowball) 4½in x 4½in (11.3cm x 11.3cm)

Finished size of quilt 74½in x 88in (189.2cm x 223.4cm)

I have also included the measurements for an alternate size using larger 6in x 6in (15.1cm x 15.1cm) blocks, which means fewer blocks would be needed for a double quilt.

Finished size of larger blocks (nine-patch and Snowball) 6in x 6in (15.1cm x 15.1cm)

Finished size of quilt 86in x 98in (218.4cm x 248.8cm)

Fabric Requirements

For the double bed quilt using the smaller 4½in x 4½in (11.3cm x 11.3cm) blocks, you will need sixteen rows of thirteen blocks in each row – a total of 208 blocks (104 nine-patch blocks, 104 Snowball blocks).

For the double bed quilt using the larger 6in x 6in (15.1cm x 15.1cm) blocks, you will need thirteen rows of eleven blocks in each row – a total of 143 blocks (72 nine-patch blocks, 71 Snowball blocks).

Nine-patch blocks plus pieced border: about 4yd (3.68m) of assorted fabrics.

Snowball main fabric: 2¼yd (2.06m).

Snowball corners: 1¼yd (1.14m) of either one fabric or an assortment.

Borders: 21in (53.3cm) for the inner border and 1yd (91.4cm) for the wide outer border.

Decorative edging: this uses a lot of fabric but is a good way of getting rid of left-overs. It is made from 4in x 4in (10cm x 10cm) squares folded into triangles –160 squares for the smaller quilt and 192 for the larger quilt.

Using the Smaller Blocks to Make the Quilt

Construction
Making the Nine-patch Blocks

You will need 104 nine-patch blocks for the quilt.

1 Sort the chosen collection of fabrics (*not* the main fabric for the Snowball block) into pairs that look good together. From each pair cut four squares from one fabric and five squares from the other fabric, each 2in x 2in (5cm x 5cm). Arrange them in a nine-patch as in Fig 1.

2 Stitch together the top row of three squares using exact ¼in (6mm) seams. Press the seams to one side, ironing from the front.

3 Stitch together the second row of three squares, pressing the seams in the opposite direction to those of row 1. Stitch together the third row of squares and press the seams in the opposite direction to those of row 2 (Fig 2). This way, the seams will lock together when the three rows are joined to make the nine-patch.

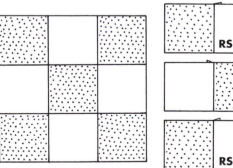

Fig 1　　　　*Fig 2*

'My collection of Civil War prints worked well with a tea-dyed plain fabric for the Snowball pattern.
This is the first time I had attempted the Prairie Points edging, which I thoroughly enjoyed.'
Collie Parker

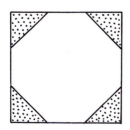

4 Stitch together the three rows, matching seams carefully (Fig 3). Press the seams to one side, ironing from the front.

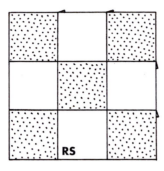

Fig 3

Tip

Each block should measure 5in x 5in (12.6cm x 12.6cm) at this stage. Make one block first so that you can check the measurements. If your block does not match this measurement, adjust the seam allowance when making the second block until you get the correct sizing. You can do some stretching out with a steam iron, but it is a good idea to sort out your seam allowance at the start rather than after you have made all 104 blocks!

Making the Snowball Blocks

You will need 104 Snowball blocks for the quilt.

5 From the fabric chosen for the main part of the Snowball blocks cut 104 squares of fabric, each 5in x 5in (12.6cm x 12.6cm). If you do not have enough fabric, introduce a complementary second fabric and alternate it with the first fabric or use it for the final row of Snowball blocks around the outer edges of the quilt.

6 Each block needs four corners, either in one fabric throughout or in a variety of fabrics to give a more scrappy effect (Fig 4). There is a painless way of adding these corner triangles to the block that is easy and accurate, if slightly wasteful of fabric. For each corner triangle cut a 2in x 2in (5cm x 5cm) square of fabric. Cut 416 squares for the quilt.

Fig 4

7 Place one square of corner fabric on to a corner of a cut Snowball square right sides facing, matching edges carefully (Fig 5). Pin it in position.

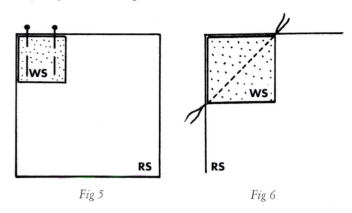

Fig 5   *Fig 6*

8 Stitch across the pinned square diagonally from corner to corner (Fig 6). To mark the line to be stitched draw a line on the wrong side of the fabric square with a sharp marking pencil. Alternatively, stick a strip of masking tape on the sewing machine plate with one edge level with the needle (Fig 7). Place the corner of the fabric under the needle and position the opposite corner exactly on top of the edge of the masking tape (Fig 8). Keep the bottom corner positioned on the edge of the masking tape at all times as you stitch.

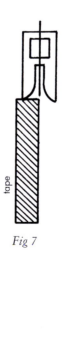

Fig 7

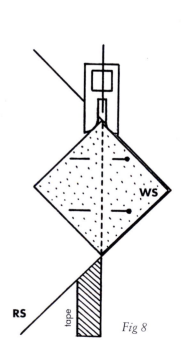

Fig 8

Trim the excess fabric ¼in (6mm) beyond the stitching line (Fig 9). The trimmed corners could be used later in a smaller project. . . possibly. . . . Press back the triangle of fabric to make the corner of the square block, pressing the seam out towards the corner (Fig 10). Add the other three corners to the block in the same way (Fig 11). Make all the Snowball blocks by adding corners in this way.

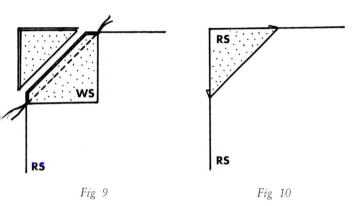

Fig 9   Fig 10

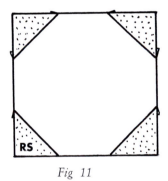

Fig 11

9 Arrange the blocks as shown in the photograph of Collie Parker's quilt on page 59. There are thirteen blocks in each horizontal row and sixteen rows of blocks to make the quilt. Pin and stitch the top row of thirteen blocks together with the usual ¼in (6mm) seam. Press the seams to one side, ironing from the front.

10 Pin and stitch the second row of thirteen blocks together. Press the seams in the opposite direction to those of row 1, ironing from the front. Continue to pin and stitch each row, pressing the seams in alternate directions to help lock the seams.

11 Join the rows together, matching the seams carefully. Press seams to one side from the front.

Using the Larger Blocks to Make the Quilt
Construction
Making the Nine-patch Blocks

Seventy-two nine-patch blocks are needed for the quilt. Follow the instructions given on page 58, steps 1–4, for making the nine-patch blocks in the smaller size but cut the squares 2½in x 2½in (6.2cm x 6.2cm). The nine-patch blocks should measure 6½in x 6½in (16.4cm x 16.4cm).

Making the Snowball Blocks

Seventy-one Snowball blocks are needed for the quilt. Follow the instructions given on page 60 for making the Snowball blocks in the smaller size but cut the main Snowball square 6½in x 6½in (16.4cm x 16.4cm) and the corner squares 2½in x 2½in (6.2cm x 6.2cm).

1 Arrange the blocks as shown in Fig 12. There are eleven blocks in each horizontal row and thirteen rows of blocks to make the quilt. Pin and stitch the top row of eleven blocks together with the usual ¼in (6mm) seam. Press the seams to one side, ironing from the front.

Fig 12

2 Pin and stitch the second row of eleven blocks together. Press the seams in the opposite direction to those of row 1, ironing from the front. Continue to pin and stitch each row, pressing the seams in alternate directions to help lock the seams.

3 Join the rows together, matching the seams carefully. Press seams to one side from the front.

Adding Borders

A border of the main Snowball fabric was added to the quilt first. For the quilt made from the smaller block use 2in (5cm) wide cut strips, and for the quilt made from the larger block use 2½in (6.2cm) wide cut strips (see Bordering a Quilt page 117). The second border continues to use up the left-overs from the main quilt. The design is a continuous band of different half-square triangles joined together (Fig 13), each square the same as the squares used for the nine-patch blocks in the quilt. The squares can be easily constructed as described below.

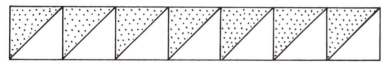

Fig 13

1 From all the chosen fabrics cut squares 2⅜in (5.9cm) for the smaller size and 2⅞in (7.2cm) for the larger size.

2 Place two different squares together with right sides facing, matching the edges carefully. Draw a diagonal line on the top fabric using a sharp marking pencil (Fig 14). Pin the two squares together ready for stitching.

3 Machine a line of stitching on *each* side of the drawn diagonal line at a distance of exactly ¼in (6mm), using the usual smaller stitch (Fig 15). A series of pinned squares can be stitched one after the other on the machine to save time and thread. Cut threads to separate stitched squares after sewing.

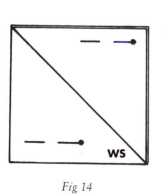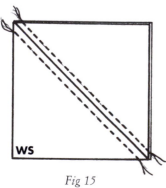

Fig 14   *Fig 15*

4 Cut along the drawn line on each stitched square. Each half is now a pieced square made of two triangles of the two different fabrics (Fig 16). Press each square from the front with the seams towards the darker fabric. Trim back the overhanging seam allowance at either end of the seam to make them level with the other fabric edges (Fig 17). The two squares will be identical so need to be used well apart from each other in the border.

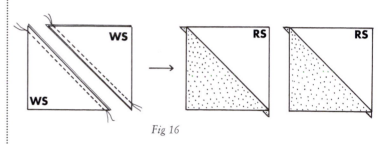

Fig 16

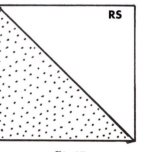

Fig 17

5 To make the border around the quilt about 182 pieced squares are needed for the smaller size quilt and 152 for the larger size. The same number of squares should be cut to use in the piecing of the border, as two squares stitched together produce two pieced squares after stitching and cutting. Make the pieced squares as described above.

For the smaller block stitch fifty pieced squares together into a strip. This should fit one side of the quilt. If it does not fit exactly, adjust the seams or steam-iron the strip until it fits the quilt. Make another strip of fifty pieced squares for the other long side of the quilt.

The quilt made from the larger block needs forty-one pieced squares stitched together for each side strip.

6 Pin and stitch a pieced strip to either side of the quilt with the usual ¼in (6mm) seam. Press seams outwards from the quilt, ironing from the front.

7 Make a strip of pieced squares for the top and bottom of the quilt. The quilt made from the smaller block needs forty-three pieced squares in each strip. The quilt from the larger block needs thirty-seven pieced squares in each strip.

8 Pin and stitch a pieced strip to the top and bottom of the quilt. Press seams outwards, ironing from the front.

9 The final wide border is made from strips cut 3½in (8.8cm) wide for the smaller block and cut 4in (10cm) wide for the larger block. For more details on adding borders see Bordering a Quilt page 117.

Quilting

Collie used a contrasting colour of quilting thread to make a well-defined quilting design on each Snowball block (Fig 18). This same thread was used to quilt the two plain borders (Fig 19). A diagonal grid was quilted in cream thread on the nine-patch blocks.

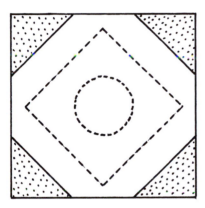

Fig 18

Fig 19

Finishing the Quilt

Collie's quilt wasn't bound in the usual way, instead a series of folded squares were used as a decorative edging. It used a great deal of fabric but is really effective.

1 About 160 folded squares are needed for the smaller size quilt and 192 for the larger quilt. Use as many of the left-over scrap fabrics as possible. Cut each square 4in x 4in (10cm x 10cm). Fold each square in half, then half again.

2 Cut each folded square in half diagonally from folded edge to folded edge, cutting off the raw edges as in Fig 20. These cut-off triangles can be joined in pairs to make squares and used later in another project.

3 Turn the backing fabric back from the quilt top and wadding (batting) and pin it out of the way. Keep the quilt top and wadding together and trim the wadding level with the edges of the quilt top.

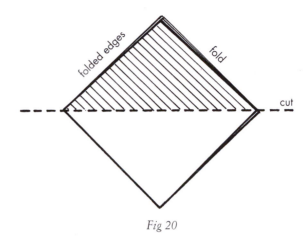

Fig 20

4 Arrange the folded triangles evenly along the four sides of the quilt as in Fig 21 with the raw edges of each triangle level with the edges of the quilt top and wadding (batting). Collie used forty-four triangles along each long side and thirty-six along the top and bottom of her quilt. For the larger quilt about fifty-one triangles are needed for each side and forty-five for the top and bottom. The triangles need to butt together exactly at each corner of the quilt (see Fig 22).

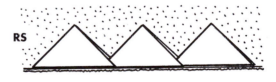

Fig 21

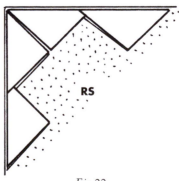

Fig 22

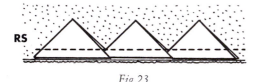

5 Sew the triangles to both the quilt top and the wadding (batting), stitching ¼in (6mm) away from the raw edges (Fig 23).

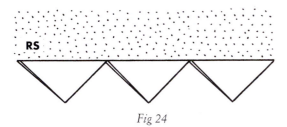

Fig 23

6 Turn the folded triangles to the outer edge of the quilt with the seams turned in towards the quilt (Fig 24). Tack (baste) around the quilt near to the seamline to keep it in place.

Fig 24

7 Turn the quilt to its wrong side and unpin the backing fabric. Trim it if necessary to about ½in (12mm) beyond the final seamline on the quilt. Fold under the edge of the backing fabric so that the folded edge is level with the seamline of the edging triangles. Slipstitch the backing fabric by hand stitching to the quilt, just covering the machined seamline (Fig 25). A line of quilting can be stitched ⅛in–¼in from the edge of the quilt to give a firmer finish if desired.

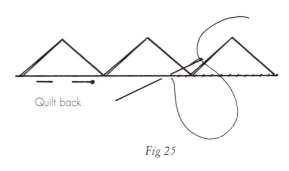

Quilt back

Fig 25

Joan Reeve's quilt used the same combination of Snowball block and Nine-patch with a limited number of fabrics placed in a balanced arrangement on the quilt. Her blocks are bigger, 9in x 9in (22.8cm x 22.8cm), with 3in (7.5cm) finished squares for the nine-patch and a 9½in (24.1cm) cut square for the Snowball block. The squares for the corners of the Snowball were cut 3½in x 3½in (8.8cm x 8.8cm). The quilt is less dense than Collie's with a greater emphasis on the quilting in the larger Snowball blocks.

'My Snowball quilt was made to replace a much-loved antique quilt on our bed, so I wanted to replicate the faded, old-fashioned look with calico and flowers. It is machine-pieced and quilted, with hand-quilted central motifs.'

Joan Reeve

All Triangles Scrap Quilt

Collie Parker's quilt (right) is built up from a simple square block – one light triangle joined to one dark triangle. The effectiveness of the design depends on using as many fabrics as possible in two groups, one of light tones and one of dark. The starting point is the sorting of the fabrics into these two groups. There is no difficulty with classifying obvious lights and darks: the problems come with the 'in–betweens'. Put these into a 'possibles' pile and deal with them after the other fabrics have been grouped (see Tip below).

Finished size of block 3in x 3in (7.5cm x 7.5cm)

Finished size of quilt 96in x 96in (243.7cm x 243.7cm)

Fabric Requirements

Because the quilt is pure random scraps, fabric amounts do not have to be a consideration. Just start cutting and stitching and see how big the quilt can get.

About 4½yd (205.7cm) assorted light fabrics for the triangles. About 4½yd (205.7cm) assorted dark fabrics for the triangles.

Border and Binding: 3yd (274.3cm). A 3in–4in (7.5cm–10cm) border for a bed quilt can be cut from 1yd (91.3cm) of fabric, while 1½yd (1.37m) would give a wider border with just one central join on each side.

Backing: 98in x 98in (250cm x 250cm).

Tip

Some fabrics 'in-between' light and dark might work in either group, but a decision must be made. Place the fabric under consideration with the other fabrics in the group to see if it will blend in and not stand out as a total stranger. Half-closing your eyes to view the fabrics can help you see the possibilities

Construction

1 Cut the chosen fabrics into strips ⅞in (2.1cm) larger than the chosen size of finished square for the design, i.e., for a 3in (7.5cm) finished square cut strips 3⅞in (9.7cm), for a 4in (10cm) finished square cut strips 4⅞in (12.3cm). Cut the strips into squares either 3⅞in (9.7cm) or 4⅞in (12.3cm).

2 Place a dark square on to a light square, right sides facing and with edges exactly matching. Pin the squares together. Draw a diagonal line across the top fabric, using a sharp marking pencil (Fig 1).

3 Machine a line of stitching on *either* side of the drawn diagonal line at a distance of exactly ¼in (6mm) using a slightly smaller stitch than usual (Fig 2). If you have a strip of tape stuck to your machine as a stitching guide you will not be able to see it through the layers of fabric, so another way of stitching accurately must be found – see Tip below.

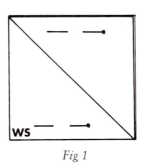
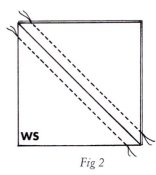

Fig 1   *Fig 2*

Tip

To machine stitch a line on either side of a drawn line at exactly ¼in (6mm), try the following:

❖ Use a special ¼in (6mm) foot on the machine;

❖ If your machine has the facility, move the needle until the distance between it and the side of your usual machine foot is exactly ¼in (6mm);

❖ Draw in a stitching line ¼in (6mm) away from the diagonal line on both sides, using a different colour marking pencil to avoid confusion.

4 Stitch down one side ¼in (6mm) from the marked line on the pinned squares, stitching them one after the other on the machine to save time and thread (Fig 3 overleaf).

5 Take the stitched squares off the machine without cutting linking threads. Turn the string of squares round and, beginning with the last square, stitch a ¼in (6mm) seam on the other side of the marked line on each square (Fig 4). Cut the threads to separate the squares after sewing.

Once the colour teams have been sorted, do not agonize over individual fabrics, just use them without careful matching and arranging. Some quilters find working in this random way almost impossible, but do persevere. There is a heady freedom in just stitching two triangles together without any thought of whether they look good together as a pair. Collie Parker sorted her fabric just into lights and darks, not colour.

'Making this all triangles quilt gave me the ideal opportunity to use my collection of plaids and stripes. The challenge was to mix the lights and darks effectively.' **Collie Parker**

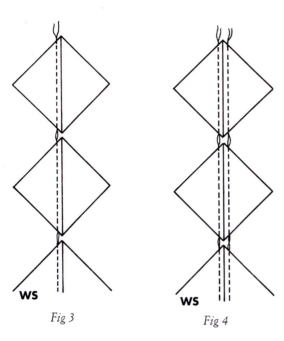

WS   WS

Fig 3   *Fig 4*

6 Cut along each drawn line between the stitched lines on each square (Fig 5). Open out each square and press it from the front, ironing the seam towards the darker fabric. Trim back the overhanging seam allowance at either end of the seam to make them level with the other edges. You will have two identical squares (Fig 6) that can be used in different places in the quilt.

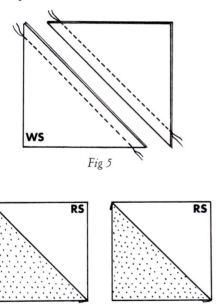

WS

Fig 5

RS   RS

Fig 6

Tip
There is another way of cutting and pairing half-square triangles using a 45° ruler and strips of fabric (see Rulers to Make the Job Easier page 126).

7 Arrange sixteen pieced light and dark squares in a block as in Fig 7. If you are using 3in (7.5cm) finished squares the block should measure 12½in x 12½in (31.7cm x 31.7cm) after stitching. If you are using 4in (10cm) finished squares the block should measure 16½in x 16½in (41.8cm x 41.8cm) after stitching.

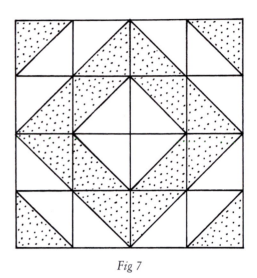

Fig 7

8 Make as many blocks as you need for your project. Arrange the blocks in the design to check that the fabrics are well balanced and that two identical fabrics aren't next to each other in the quilt. Sometimes this cannot be avoided but it is best not to let it happen too often.

9 Collie's quilt uses seven blocks in each horizontal row and seven rows of blocks to make the quilt. Pin and stitch the top row of seven blocks together with the usual ¼in (6mm) seam. Press the seams to one side, ironing from the front.

10 Pin and stitch the second row of seven blocks together. Press the seams in the opposite direction to those of row 1, ironing from the front. Continue to pin and stitch each row, pressing the seams in alternate directions to help lock the seams.

11 Join the rows together, matching seams carefully. Press seams to one side from the front.

Adding Borders

A border cut 6½in (16.4cm) wide was added on all four sides of the quilt (see Bordering a Quilt page 117). The same fabric was used to bind the quilt.

Quilting

A simple quilting line ¼in (6mm) from the seamlines accentuates the square-on-point design (Fig 8). Collie quilted her design by hand. She also hand-pieced the quilt as she doesn't even own a sewing machine!

Kate Riddleston controlled the colour placement in her design, grouping the reds and blues while keeping the lights more random.

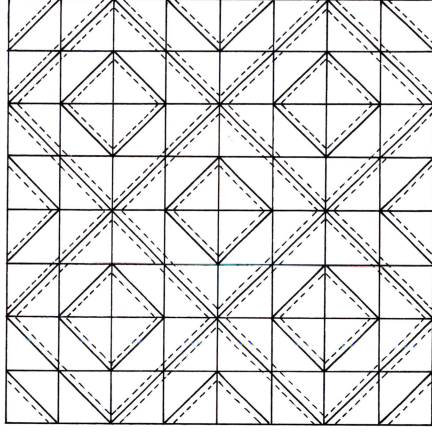

Fig 8

Quilts from Squares & Triangles

Lindy Ward's quilt used half-square triangles stitched in pairs to make squares. She used a wide range of light and dark greens together with light and dark reds. The small squares combined a light triangle with a dark triangle and measured 2in x 2in (5cm x 5cm) finished size. The larger squares used the same combination of a light and dark triangle and measured 6in x 6in (15.1cm x 15.1cm) finished size. The blocks were arranged on point and set into a rich background fabric. The block is drawn here.

'My son saw the design of this quilt which was in blue fabrics. "I like that", he said, "but would like it in red and green" and then left for university. Fortunately, I made a double-bed size as I finished it one week before he got married. They have decorated their bedroom to complement the quilt.' **Lindy Ward**

Quilts with Appliqué

Both quilts in this section combine pieced blocks with appliqué and are a good way to use a variety of different fabrics in the one design. My collection of fabrics had been deliberately gathered for years ready for such a project, while Julia Reed's quilt on page 83 was made from her huge collection of autumn-coloured fabrics. There are two different appliqué techniques described: the first quilt uses blanket-stitched appliqué, to which I am totally addicted, and the second is made using freezer paper and hand stitching.

Flowery Appliqué Quilt

For years I have been collecting 1930s reproduction fabrics, planning to make a quilt based on my grandmother's tea set that I remember so fondly from my childhood. It had a design of fat flowers on a buttery-yellow background, so finding the same shade in a plain fabric was all I needed to make a start. The problem with collecting fabric for a specific project is that you just keep on buying it 'in case I don't have enough for the quilt'. I now have enough of that Thirties range of fabrics to make a dormitory of quilts, yet recently, when a student of mine offered to buy some I found it impossible to let it go.

My design (right) combines a nine-patch block of assorted squares with an appliquéd block. The appliqué uses blanket stitch around the edges which have been first stuck into place with fusible web. A quilt by Betty Summers (see page 81) has the same general design but combines the flower appliqué with cherries and uses very different fabrics.

Finished size of blocks 9in x 9in (22.8cm x 22.8cm)

Finished size of quilt 64in x 92in (231cm x 162.5cm)

Fabric Requirements

Background and border: twenty squares of fabric each cut 9½in x 9½in (24.1cm x 24.1cm).

Two side borders cut 9½in x 72½in (24.1cm x 184cm) and two top and bottom border strips cut 9½in x 45½in (24.1cm x 116cm).

Total background fabric: 3½yds (3.20m).

Flowers, nine-patch squares and binding: assorted fabrics, as many as you can gather, in total 3yd (2.74m) plus ½yd (45.7cm) of green for the leaves.

Wadding (batting): 66in x 94in (167.6cm x 238.7cm).

Backing: 66in x 94in (167.6cm x 238.7cm).

Thicker thread for the blanket stitch appliqué – I used Gütermann silk thread.

Iron-on fusible web: 1yd (91.4cm) – I used Bondaweb, known in the USA as Wonder-Under.

Construction
Making the Nine-patch Blocks

You will need twenty-four nine-patch blocks for the quilt.

1 From the chosen collection of fabrics (not the background fabric) cut 216 squares each 3½in x 3½in (8.8cm x 8.8cm). Sort these into groups of nine squares, trying not to use the same fabric twice in each group.

2 To make the top row for each block, stitch together three cut squares, using an exact ¼in (6mm) seam. Press the

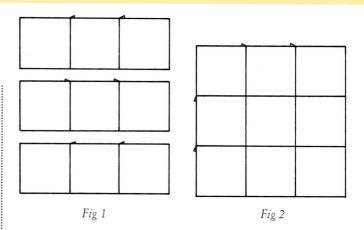

Fig 1   *Fig 2*

seams to one side, ironing from the front.

3 Stitch together the second row of three squares, pressing the seams in the opposite direction to those of row 1. Stitch together the third row of squares and press the seams in the opposite direction to those of row 2 (Fig 1). This way the seams will lock together when the three rows are joined to make the nine-patch.

4 Stitch together the three rows, matching seams carefully. Press the seams to one side, ironing from the front (Fig 2).

Tip

Each four-patch block should measure 9½in x 9½in (24.1cm x 24.1cm). Make just one block first so that you can check the measurements. If your block does not match this measurement, adjust the seam allowance when making the second block until you get the correct sizing. You can do some stretching out with a steam iron, but it is a good idea to sort out your seam allowance at the start rather than after you have made all twenty-four nine-patch blocks.

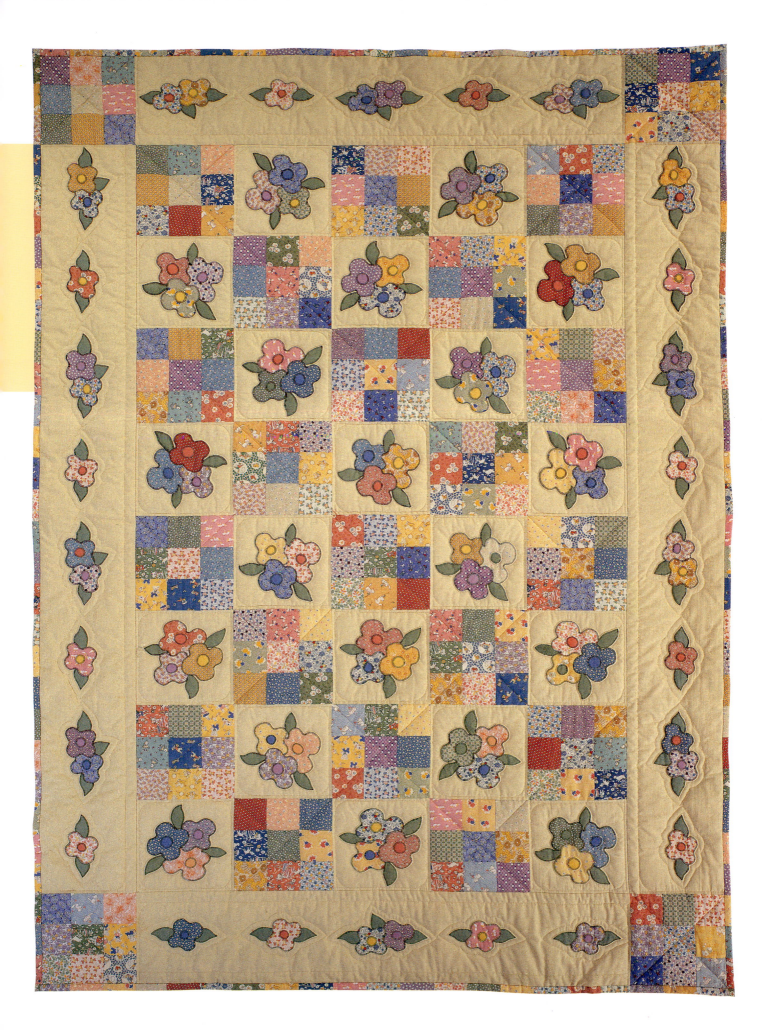

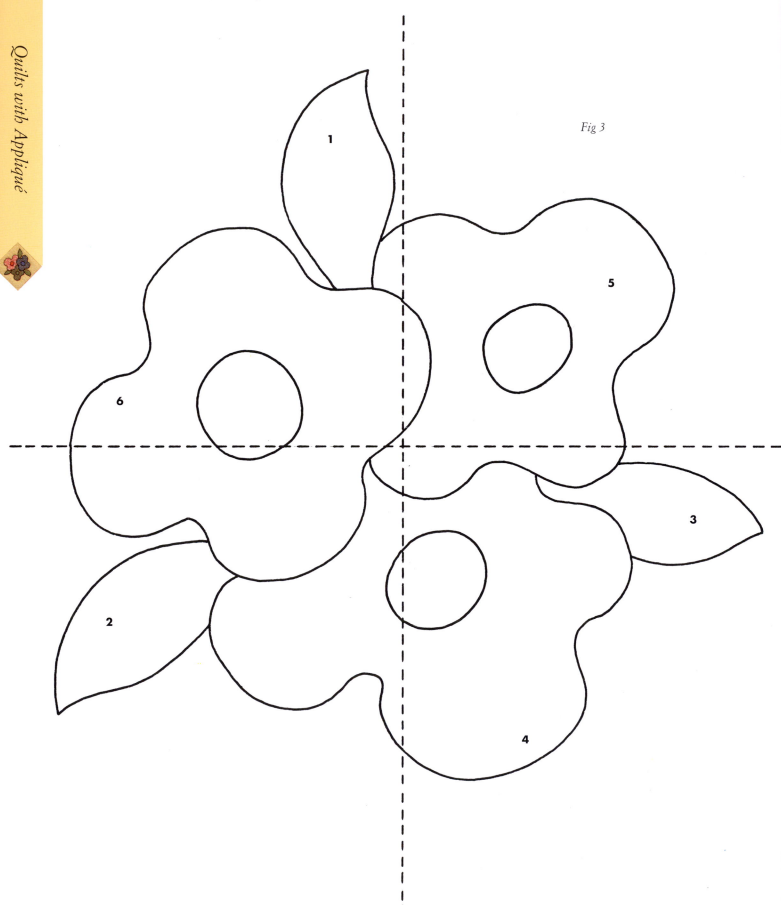

Fig 3

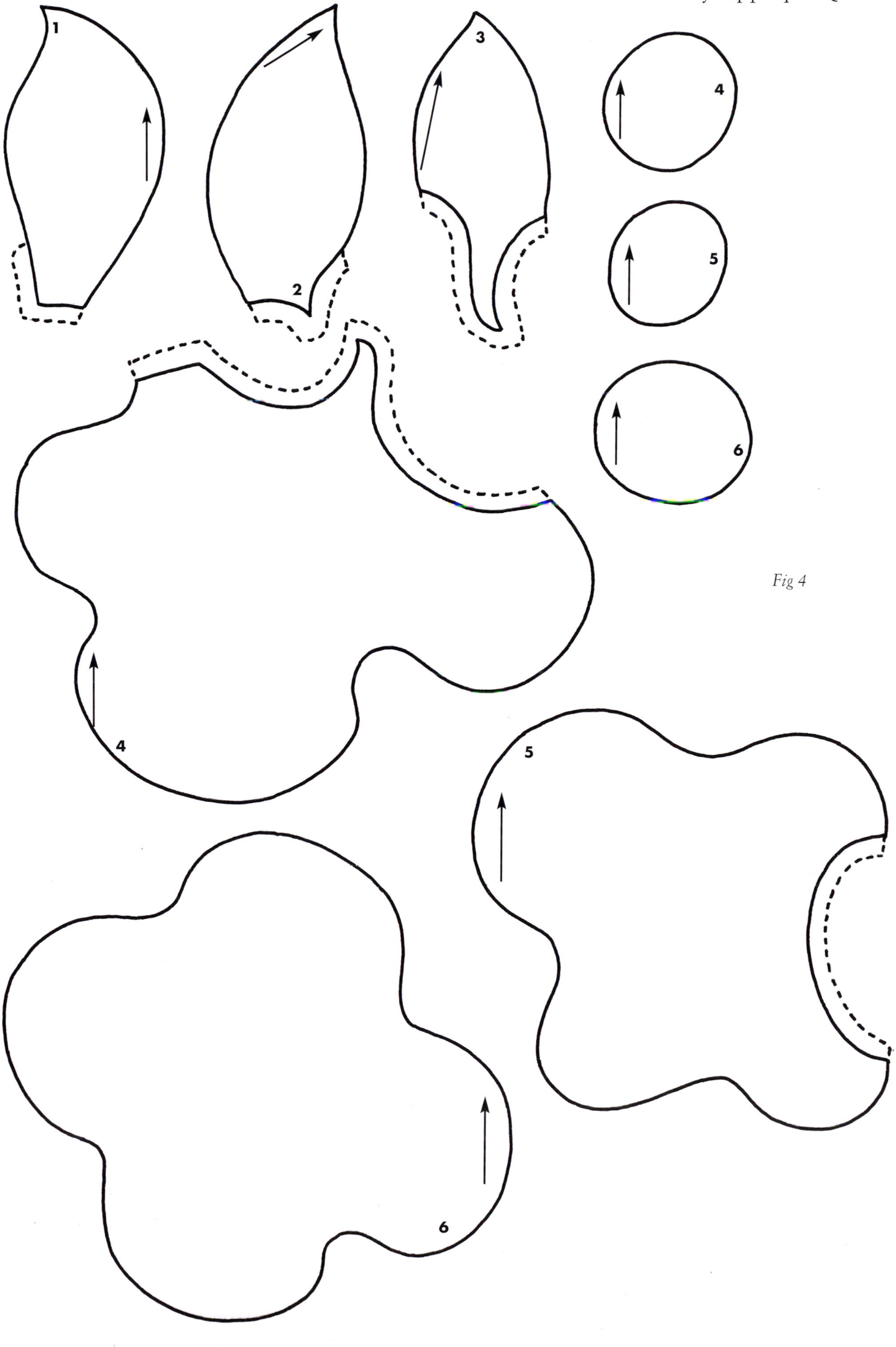

1

2

3

4

5

6

4

5

6

Fig 4

Making the Appliqué Blocks

5 From the background fabric cut twenty squares, each 9½in x 9½in (24.1cm x 24.1cm). Fold each square lightly into four. Use the fold lines as a guide for positioning the bunch of flowers – the dotted lines in Fig 3 on page 74 should match the fold lines in each square of fabric.

6 On to each square of fabric trace the bunch of flowers design shown in Fig 3. Trace very lightly just *inside* the drawn outline so that when the appliqué pieces are positioned on the background the drawn lines are hidden. I use a soft pencil for marking on light-coloured fabric and a white watercolour pencil on darker fabric.

Blanket Stitch Appliqué

This technique uses a fusible web such as Bondaweb to stick down the raw edges of the appliqué pieces on to the background fabric before stitching around the design with blanket stitch. The Bondaweb is used to stick only the outer ⅛in (3mm) of each appliqué piece – this avoids the thick, stiff layers usually associated with fusible work.

7 When using fusible web the design must be reversed. Fig 4 on page 75 gives each reversed shape to make the bunch of flowers design. The dotted lines should be included – they are areas where one shape is overlapped by another.

Tip

Beware! Fusible webs are a disaster if they get transferred by a hot iron to the base of the iron or ironing board, spreading nasty black marks where you don't want them. To guard against this, place a sheet of greaseproof or non-stick paper on the ironing board before you start and use another sheet between the iron and the fusible web as you stick.

8 Using the fusible web: Place the fusible web *smooth side uppermost* over the shapes in Fig 4 and trace each section, including any dotted areas. Mark the grain-line arrows and the numbers on the tracing, keeping these at the very edge of the shape rather than in the centre, as the centre area of fusible web will be removed later. The shapes can be traced closer together but leave about ½in (12mm) between each traced shape to make cutting out easier.

9 Cut out each traced shape roughly ¼in (6mm) beyond the outer drawn line (Fig 5). Carefully cut out the central area of fusible web and remove it, leaving only about ⅛in (3mm) inside the drawn line (Fig 6). The removed pieces of fusible web can be used for smaller shapes like the flower centres, or kept for later projects.

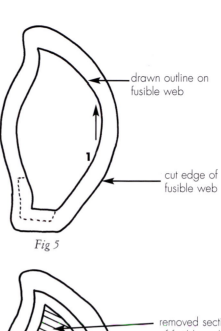

Fig 5

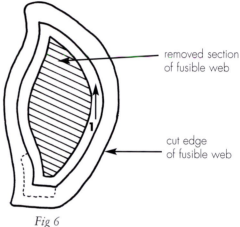

Fig 6

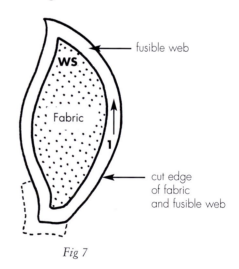

Fig 7

10 Place each cut piece of fusible web *rough side downwards* on the *wrong* side of the chosen fabric, matching the grain-line arrow with the grain or weave of the fabric. Press with a hot iron to stick the web to the fabric. Use the green fabric for all leaves and an assortment of fabrics for the flowers and their centres.

11 Now cut accurately along the drawn line through both web and fabric. Include in the cut-out shape any dotted area (Fig 7).

12 Remove the paper backing. Position the shape *right* side up, glue side *down* in the correct place on the background square. Iron it on to the fabric to stick it down.

13 Building up the design: Place each bonded shape in position, glue side *down*, on the background square, beginning with the three leaves. Press the shapes with the iron to stick them in place. Position and iron down the three flowers, starting with the largest (number 4), then 5 and finally flower 6. Position the centre circle of each flower by eye, matching the grain of the fabric circle with the grain of the flower. Iron each centre into place. The designs can now be blanket stitched in place by hand or machine.

14 Hand stitching the design: Use a slightly thicker thread than usual (I like the Gütermann silk thread) and a fine sewing needle like a Sharps 9 or 10. Black is often used to outline this type of design, but any choice of colour thread will be fine. Using a blanket stitch, stitch the leaves first, then the flowers and finally the flower centres. Try to keep the stitches all the same length, about ³⁄₁₆in (4 or 5mm), and evenly spaced (Fig 8). When turning sharp corners like the points of the leaves, make one extra tiny stitch on the spot at the corner to keep that long corner stitch in place (Fig 9). Before stitching around the circles that make the flower centres, the layers of the appliqué may be reduced by turning the whole piece over and cutting away the background

areas within the blanket-stitched edges ¼in (6mm) away from the stitching. This is not obligatory, so if your nerve fails you, just leave all the layers intact. I like to cut away the back layers to make quilting easier and to give the quilt more life.

15 Machine stitching the design: Many machines do an excellent blanket stitch, though you may need to practise stitching around corners and so on. It may be easier to stick the first leaf in position and machine blanket stitch around it before sticking on the next leaf. Stitching each section of the design before the next piece is stuck into place will make the start and finish on each shape less obvious.

Assembling the Blocks

16 Once the twenty appliqué blocks have been completed lay out twenty of the nine-patch squares and all twenty appliqué blocks in the arrangement shown in Fig 10. Move them around until you are happy with the balance of colour. The appliquéd squares can be arranged as in Fig 3 or some turned through 90° or 180° to vary the look of the design.

17 Stitch the top row of five blocks together using a ¼in (6mm) seam. Press seams to one side, ironing from the front.

18 Stitch row 2 together. Press the seams in the opposite direction to row 1. Continue to stitch each horizontal row of blocks together, pressing the seams in the opposite

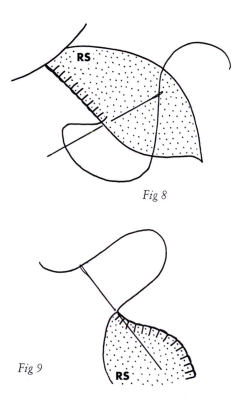

Fig 8

Fig 9

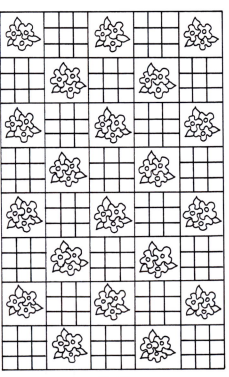

Fig 10

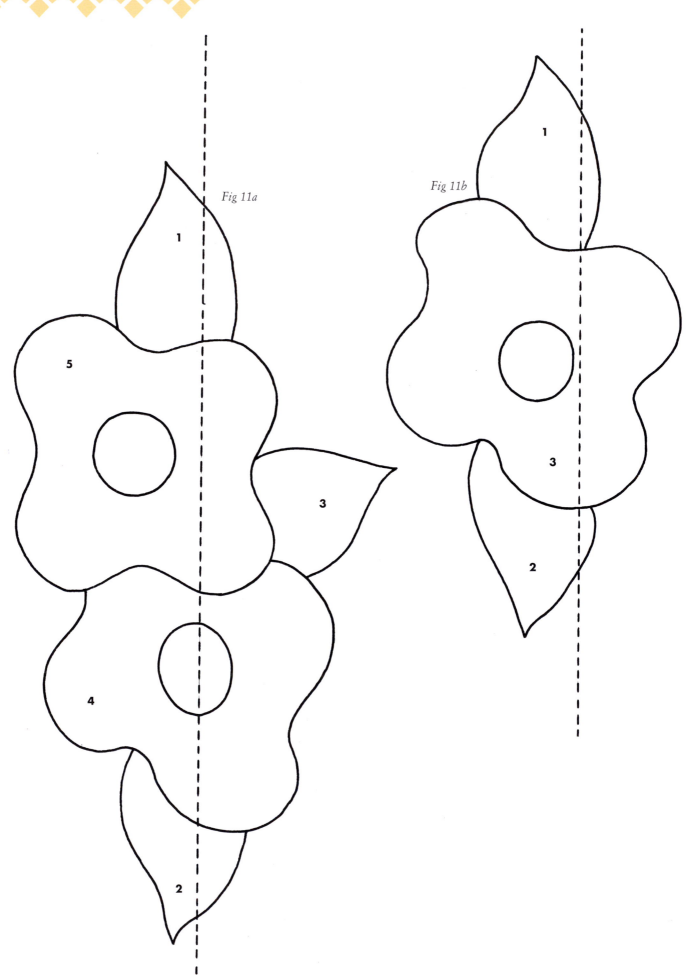

Fig 11a

Fig 11b

direction to the previous row. This means that the seams will butt together when the rows are joined, making them easier to match and stitch.

19 Stitch the rows together, row by row, matching seams carefully. Press the seams all in one direction, ironing from the front.

Making the Borders

1 Measure the quilt in both directions, across the centre rather than at the edge. It should measure 72¼in x 45½in (184cm x 116cm). If this is not the case (let's face it, it seldom is), try some rescuing strategies. In many cases the quilt is smaller than it should be, in which case try steam-pressing it from the front to pull it out as much as possible. If the quilt is larger than it should be try taking in some of the seams to reduce it. Alternatively you could just keep the quilt the size it is and cut the border strips to match it.

2 Cut two long strips of background fabric for side borders 9½in x 72¼in (24.1cm x 184cm) and two strips of background fabric for top and bottom borders 9½in x 45½in (24.1cm x 116cm), or in lengths to match your quilt if its measurements are not the same as these.

3 The bunches of flowers used for the appliqué on the border are shown in Figs 11a and 11b (left). Trace four of each design on to tracing paper and cut them out. Arrange the eight shapes alternately along one long border strip as shown in Fig 12 above.

4 Pin the traced shapes on to the background to use as a guide for positioning when tracing each one from Figs 11a and 11b. Remove each paper tracing in turn as the shapes are traced on to the background strip. Trace lightly just inside the drawn outlines as before.

5 Trace the arrangements of flowers on the opposite side border strip to give a mirror image on the sides. In the same way, arrange and pin five traced flower shapes on the top border strip. Alternate designs 11a and 11b as in Fig 13.

6 Trace the five outlines on to the strip, tracing lightly just inside the drawn outlines. Reverse the arrangement of 11a and 11b as in Fig 14.

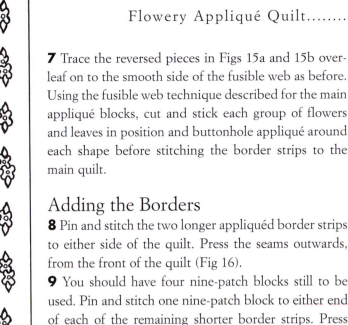

Fig 12

7 Trace the reversed pieces in Figs 15a and 15b overleaf on to the smooth side of the fusible web as before. Using the fusible web technique described for the main appliqué blocks, cut and stick each group of flowers and leaves in position and buttonhole appliqué around each shape before stitching the border strips to the main quilt.

Adding the Borders

8 Pin and stitch the two longer appliquéd border strips to either side of the quilt. Press the seams outwards, from the front of the quilt (Fig 16).

9 You should have four nine-patch blocks still to be used. Pin and stitch one nine-patch block to either end of each of the remaining shorter border strips. Press seams from the front towards the border fabric (Fig 17).

10 Stitch the top and bottom borders to the quilt, matching seams carefully. Press the seams towards the outer edge of the quilt, ironing from the front.

Fig 16

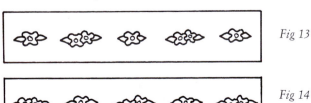

Fig 13

Fig 14

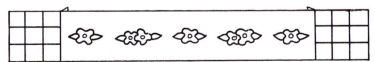

Fig 17

Fig 15a

Fig 15b

Fig 18

Quilting

I machine quilted diagonally across the nine-patch blocks and then hand quilted the appliquéd blocks. I quilted around the flower bunches about ¼in (6mm) away and also around the flower centres. To finish off each appliqué block I hand quilted a frame ¼in (6mm) within the outer edge of each background square and gave it a 1930s look by adding an extra curved quilting line at each corner of the square

(Fig 18). The border strips were quilted in the same way, but increasing the gap between the flower blocks and the surrounding quilting to ½in (12mm).

To bind the quilt, left-over scraps from the flowers and nine-patches were cut into 2½in (6.3cm) wide strips and joined together as a multi-fabric binding. For more ideas on finishing and quilting see pages 117 and 122.

'This is my first quilt, made for my eldest grandchild Anna. I first planned to use Sunbonnet Sue designs for the appliqué but finally chose the flowers and cherries so that the quilt would last through her childhood and even beyond that.' **Betty Summers**

Daisy Chain Appliqué Quilt

Pat Mitchell's All Square quilt on page 11 uses large squares, four-patch blocks and nine-patch blocks to create an overall quilt design. Julia Reed's Daisy Chain quilt (right) uses a block of similar squares and alternates it with a hand-appliquéd daisy block and a quilted daisy. When the blocks are joined the squares form a series of diagonal chains across the quilt which frame and separate the appliquéd and quilted blocks. The centre 9in x 9in (22.8cm x 22.8cm) finished square that holds the appliqué or quilting could be replaced with a different appliqué design or even a pieced block like Ohio Star to create a completely different quilt. The chain block would give a diagonal setting to whatever was chosen to use in the alternating square, which is unusual and really effective.

Finished size of block   9in x 9in (22.8cm x 22.8cm)

Finished size of quilt   79in x 79in (206cm x 206cm)

Fabric Requirements

Assorted scrap fabrics are needed for the quilt as shown – 2½yd (2.28m) for the chain blocks, appliquéd daisies, the border of pieced squares and the binding. In Julia's quilt both the appliqué and the chain are made from scraps of as many fabrics as possible in a yellow/orange/brown colour range. Your collection of fabrics could be in any colour range you like, even using one group of fabrics for the appliquéd daisies and another collection in a different colour for the chains.

Background fabric: 3½yd (3.20m).

Wadding (batting): 81in x 81in (205.6cm x 205.6cm).

Backing fabric: 81in x 81in (205.6cm x 205.6cm).

Construction
Making the Chain Blocks

Twenty-four blocks are needed for the design.

1 From the background fabric cut ninety-six squares each 3½in x 3½in (8.8cm x 8.8cm).

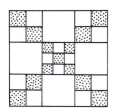

Fig 1a

Fig 1b

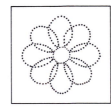

Fig 1c

Making the Four-patch Blocks

2 Ninety-six four-patch blocks are needed for the quilt. From the group of assorted scrap fabrics cut strips each 2in (5cm) wide. If your fabric pieces are long enough, cut strips about 21in (53.2cm) long. If not, cut several shorter lengths from each fabric. Match each strip with a similar length of 2in (5cm) wide background fabric.

3 Place a strip from the scrap collection with a similar strip of background fabric, right sides facing. Stitch a ¼in (6mm) seam to join the strips together, matching edges carefully and using a smaller stitch than usual (Fig 2). Open the strips out and press the seam towards the scrap fabric, ironing from the front (Fig 3).

4 Cut the joined strips vertically into 2in (5cm) wide pieces (Fig 4 overleaf). In the same way, continue to stitch pairs of strips together and cut them into pieces until 192 pieces have been cut.

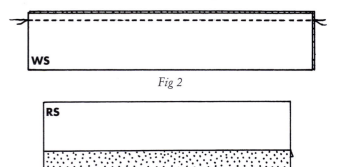

Fig 2

Fig 3

The quilt is not a full-size one but is big enough to fit a single bed or be placed on point on the top of a double bed. It can be lengthened with another row of blocks if necessary and another two rows added to the width to fit a king-size bed.

'The colours of autumn leaves always inspire me to make quilts. This quilt design should help clear the resulting heaps of scraps!' **Julia Reed**

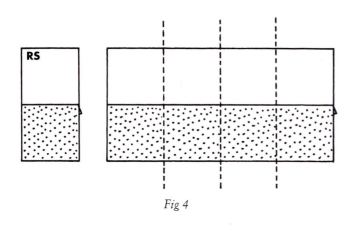

Fig 4

5 Arrange two pieces made from different scrap fabrics into a four-patch as in Fig 5. Pin and stitch the pair together, matching the centre seams carefully. Press the seam to one side, ironing from the front (Fig 6).

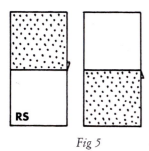 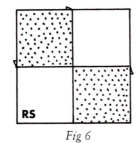

Fig 5   *Fig 6*

Tip

Each four-patch block should measure exactly 3½in x 3½in (8.8cm x 8.8cm) at this stage. Check the measurement of the first block. If it is not this size, adjust the seam allowances when making the second block until you get the right sizing. You can do some stretching out with a steam iron but it is a good idea to sort out your seam allowance at the start rather than after you have made all ninety-six blocks!

6 Continue to pin and stitch each four-patch until ninety-six four-patch blocks have been made. Time and thread can be saved if the blocks are stitched in a chain, one after the other, without taking them off the machine and only cutting the thread between each block once they are completed.

Making the Nine-patch Blocks

If the twenty-four nine-patch blocks are to be true scrap blocks, that is, all different, they have to be made from individually cut squares rather than cut from strips and speed-pieced. If you decide to make them all identical, the method for quick strip-piecing is given in the instructions for the All Square quilt on page 10, steps 1–6. Cut strips and pieces

1½in (3.7cm) wide at all times instead of 2in (5cm), as directed in the All Square quilt. The lengths for band A should be three sets of strips measuring 25in (63.4cm), a total length of 75in (190.3cm). The lengths for band B should be two sets of strips measuring 30in (76.1cm), a total length of 60in (152.2cm). This will make the required twenty-four nine-patch blocks.

7 For the scrap nine-patch blocks cut 120 squares of the scrap fabrics and 96 squares of background fabric, each 1½in x 1½in (3.7cm x 3.7cm). Take five squares of scrap fabric, all different, and four squares of background fabric and arrange them into a nine-patch (Fig 7).

8 Stitch together the top row of three squares, using an exact ¼in (6mm) seam. Press the seams towards the scrap squares, ironing from the front.

9 Stitch together the second row of three squares, pressing the seams towards the centre square of scrap fabric. Stitch together the third row of squares and press the seams towards the two scrap squares (Fig 8). This way the seams will lock together when the three rows are joined to make the nine-patch.

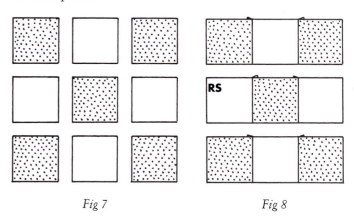

Fig 7   *Fig 8*

10 Stitch together the three rows, matching seams carefully. Press the seams out from the centre, ironing from the front (Fig 9). Check the sizing of this first block in the same way as for the four-patch blocks. It should measure 3½in x 3½in (8.8cm x 8.8cm) at this stage.

11 Now arrange and stitch together twenty-three more nine-patch blocks in the same way as described above, varying the squares of scrap fabrics as much as possible in each block.

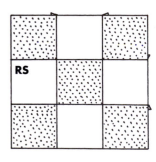

Fig 9

Assembling the Chain Blocks

12 Arrange four background 3½in (8.8cm) squares with four four-patch blocks and one nine-patch block as shown in Fig 10. Try to vary the scrap fabric squares as much as possible. Pin and stitch the nine units together row by row in the same way as for the nine-patch blocks. Press the seams of each row towards the background fabric. Finally, press the long joining seams to one side, ironing from the front. Check that all the squares are in the correct position as in Fig 1a on page 82.

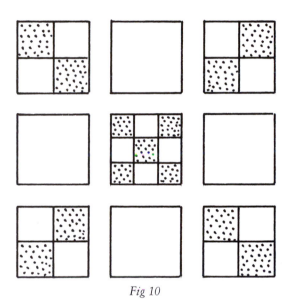

Fig 10

Making the Appliqué Blocks

13 The design drawn in Fig 11 on page 86 is half the daisy appliqué pattern. Trace it on to a large sheet of tracing paper, including the dotted lines. Now rotate the tracing paper 180° and complete the daisy by tracing, matching the dotted lines.

14 From the background fabric cut twenty-five squares, each 9½in x 9½in (24.1cm x 24.1cm). Set twelve squares aside for the quilted blocks. Fold each of the remaining thirteen squares lightly into four. Use the fold lines as a guide for positioning the traced daisy design – the dotted lines in Fig 11 should match the fold lines in each square of fabric.

15 Trace the daisy design shown in Fig 11 on to each square of fabric. Trace very lightly just inside the drawn outline so that when the appliqué pieces are positioned on the background the drawn lines are hidden. I use a soft pencil for marking on light-coloured fabric and a white watercolour pencil on darker fabric.

Freezer Paper Appliqué

I like to use freezer paper to do this type of appliqué, so my instructions are for this technique. If you prefer to needle-turn or have another favourite method of appliqué then use the petal and centre circle template shapes given in Fig 12 on page 86 and stitch the design in your own way.

16 For each daisy design trace the petal shape from Fig 12 on to the smooth side of the freezer paper twelve times. Cut out the shapes on the drawn line and iron them, *shiny side down*, on to the *wrong* side of as many different scrap fabrics as possible. Match the grain-line arrow on the freezer paper with the grain or weave of the fabrics. Cut around the freezer paper with a scant ¼in (6mm) seam allowance (Fig 13). This does not have to be carefully measured but can be cut by eye.

17 Peel the freezer paper off the fabric and replace it shiny side *up* on the *wrong* side of the fabric in exactly the same position. Pin the freezer paper on to the fabric (Fig 14). I use two pins to stop the paper moving. Do not clip the seam allowance.

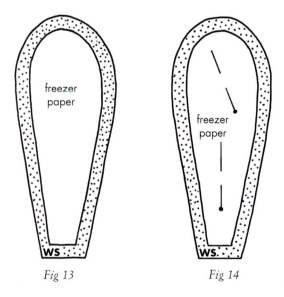

Fig 13   *Fig 14*

18 Using the side of an iron, nudge the seam allowance of fabric over on to the freezer paper, easing in the fullness a little at a time so that it sticks to the paper. Leave the bottom straight edge of fabric unturned. Don't worry too much if the iron touches the surface of the freezer paper but take care not to press any tiny pleats in the outer edge, especially on the curved top of the petal – keep the curve smooth (Fig 15 on page 87). If there are any areas you are not happy with, just peel the paper back and re-press in the correct position.

Quilts with Appliqué

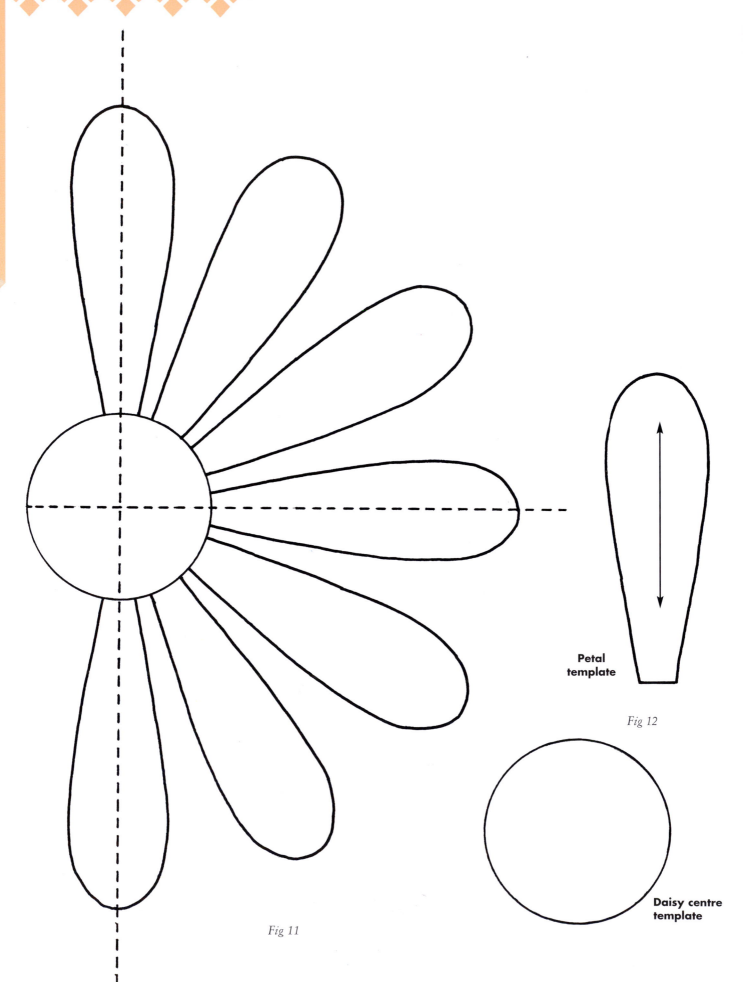

Petal
template

Fig 12

Daisy centre
template

Fig 11

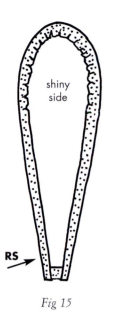

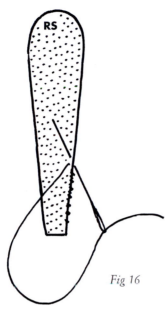

shiny side

RS

RS

Fig 15

Fig 16

19 Arrange the twelve prepared shapes on the background, checking that the balance of fabrics works well. Press the petals from the front with the iron. This will fix them on the background while you stitch each petal in place, although you may also want to pin them for added security. Using a thread in a colour to match the petal, not the background, stitch the folded curved edge in position using small, even slipstitches and beginning and ending ¼in (6mm) from the unturned edge (Fig 16).

20 Once each petal is stitched, lift up the unstitched bottom edge and see if the freezer paper can be eased out. Slide a pair of small scissors with rounded ends between the paper and the background fabric to separate them: the paper can then be pulled out using a pair of tweezers. If not, turn the square of background fabric over, cut a slit about 2in (5cm) long in the background fabric *only* down the centre behind the stitched leaf and pull the paper out through the slit, leaving the slit unstitched.

21 Stitch each petal into place and remove the freezer paper. Prepare the centre circle by tracing the circle template in Fig 12 on to freezer paper and cutting it out exactly on the drawn line. Select a fabric for the centre and iron the freezer paper circle on to the *wrong* side of the fabric. Follow the procedure given for preparing the petals with freezer paper and iron the fabric seam allowance over on to the paper circle. Position the fabric circle in the centre of the daisy design. Turn the circle so that the grain of the fabric runs parallel to the grain of the background before pressing it to fix it on to the block. Stitch it into place using thread to match the fabric of the daisy centre, not the background.

22 Turn the block to the back and use the stitch line as a guide to cut away the background fabric up to ¼in (6mm) within the stitching line of the centre circle, revealing the freezer paper below. Remove the freezer paper from the block (Fig 17). Stitch all thirteen daisy appliqué blocks in this way.

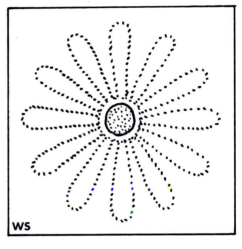

WS

Fig 17

Preparing the Quilted Blocks

It is easier to mark the remaining twelve squares of background fabric with the quilting design shown in Fig 18 on page 88 *before* they are joined to the other blocks.

23 Trace the design from Fig 18, including the fold lines, on to a large sheet of tracing paper using a strong marking pen.

24 Fold each of the squares of background fabric lightly into four. Use the fold lines as a guide for positioning the quilting design – the fold lines in Fig 18 should match the fold lines in each square of fabric.

25 Trace the quilting design on to each fabric square, marking lightly with a suitable marking pencil – I use a watercolour pencil in a shade that tones with the quilting thread.

Assembling the Blocks

26 Arrange the forty-nine blocks as in Julia's quilt, shown on page 83. Pin and stitch the top row of seven blocks together with the usual ¼in (6mm) seam. Press seams to one side, ironing from the front.

27 Pin and stitch the second row of seven blocks together. Press the seams in the opposite direction to those of row 1, ironing from the front. Continue to pin and stitch each row, pressing seams in alternate directions to help lock them.

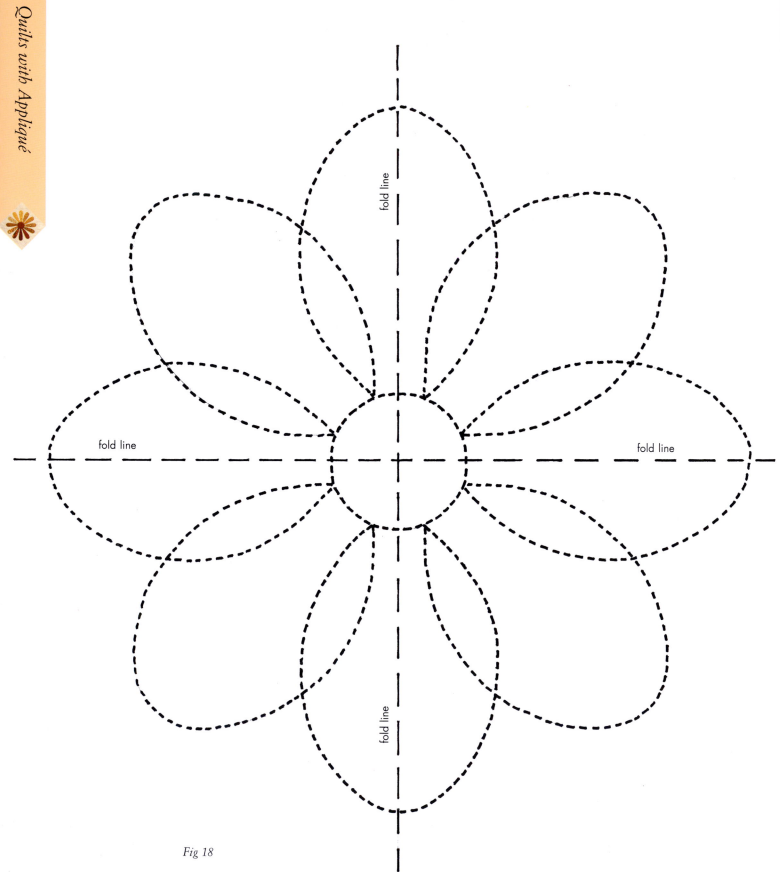

fold line

fold line

fold line

fold line

Fig 18

28 Join the rows together, matching seams carefully. Press seams to one side from the front.

Adding Borders

Julia's quilt was framed with a narrow strip of background fabric cut 2in (5cm) wide, followed by three rows of squares of scrap fabrics, each cut 2in x 2in (5cm x 5cm). A final strip of background fabric cut 2½in (6.3cm) was used to border the quilt before a multi-fabric binding of left-over strips. See Bordering a Quilt page 117.

Quilting

In addition to the twelve marked squares that were quilted in a contrasting brown thread during construction of the quilt, Julia also quilted around each appliquéd daisy, working about ⅛in (3mm) from the edge of the petals and diagonally across the chain blocks as shown in Fig 19.

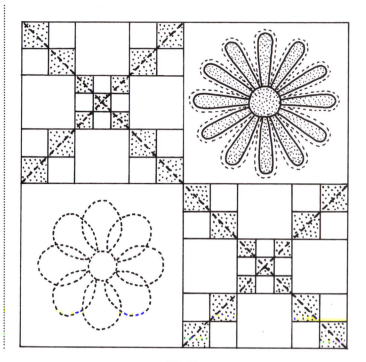

Fig 19

Use It All Up!

I have included a special section in this book on smaller projects, so that really limited amounts of saved fabric can be gathered together and used for one of the projects. These are a pleated drawstring bag, a smiley suns and stars cot quilt, a crazy quillow and a child's 'I Spy' quilt. Small quilts are very satisfying to make. They take less time and make perfect presents – a good way to reduce those piles of fabric.

Drawstring Bag

This drawstring bag is very different from the usual idea of a patchwork bag. The pleated effect of the main outer bag means that it uses a lot of fabric, but a mixture of several toning or even contrasting fabrics could be used instead of limiting it to just two outer fabrics plus a lining.

Fabric Requirements

Outer pleated section, outer bag base and binding strips: ½yd (45.6cm).

Inner pleated section and straps: 32in (81.2cm) of fabric 42in–44in (106.6cm–111.7cm) wide.

Top drawstring section: two pieces each 6¼in x 13in (15.1cm x 33cm). This could be from either of the two main fabrics or from a completely different fabric.

Lining fabric: ½yd (45.6cm).

Thin wadding (batting): for bag base 5in x 10½in (12.7cm x 26.7cm).

Two D-rings: to fit 1½in (3.8cm) width straps.

Decorative cord: two 24in (60.9cm) lengths.

Construction

1 From fabric A (the fabric used for the outer pleats) cut twenty-four strips each 1½in x 10½in (3.8cm x 26.7cm).

2 From fabric B (the fabric used for the inner pleats) cut twenty-four strips each 2½in x 10½in (6.3cm x 26.7cm).

3 With right sides facing and using a ¼in (6mm) seam, stitch one strip of fabric A to one strip of fabric B (Fig 1). Repeat this with all twenty-four pairs of strips.

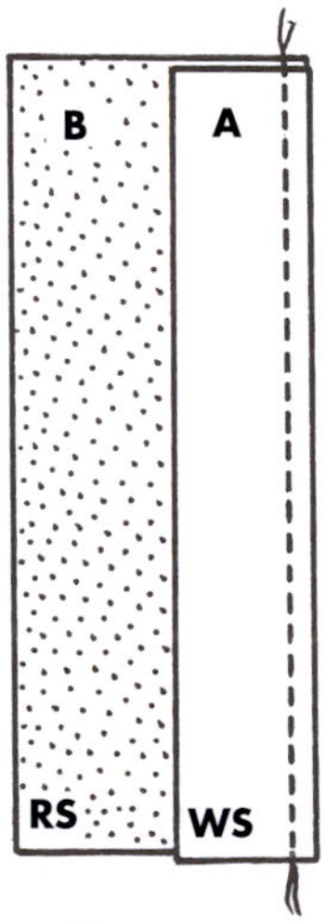

4 Stitch the pairs of strips together so that fabrics A and B alternate. Press the seams towards the narrower strips of fabric A, ironing from the front (Fig 2).

5 Pin and stitch together the first and last strips in the band to make a tube. Turn the tube right sides outwards and press the last seam towards fabric A (Fig 3).

6 With wrong sides facing and with the strip of fabric A uppermost, fold the tube on one stitched seam. Topstitch close to the edge of the fabric, using a toning thread (Fig 4). Repeat this on all the seams in the tube (Fig 5).

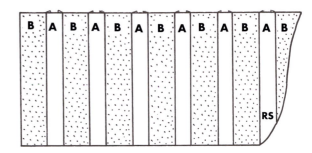

Fig 1

Fig 2

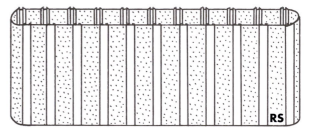

Fig 3

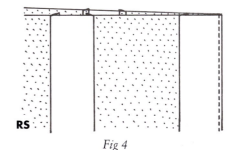

Fig 4

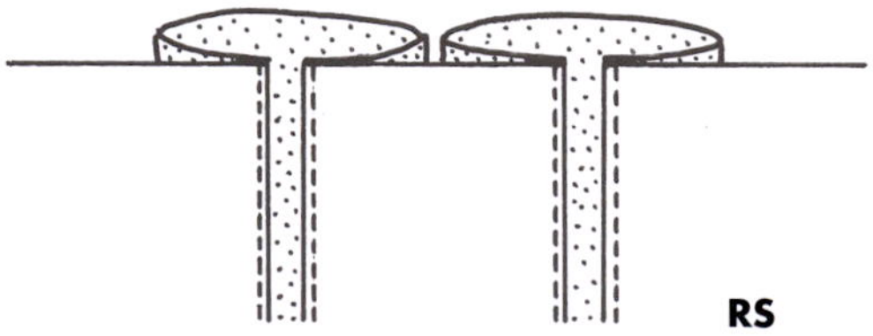

Fig 5

7 Arrange the fabric strips in flat pleats with the top-stitched edges butted together as in Fig 6. Pin the pleats in place at the top end of the tube and again at the bottom. Using a long machine stitch, sew a temporary line of stitches ¼in (6mm) from both top and bottom edges of the tube to hold the pleats in position (Fig 7). Remove the pins.

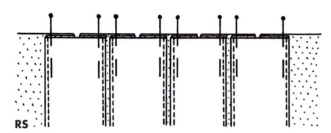

Fig 6

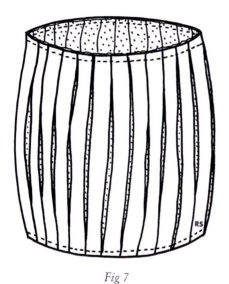

Fig 7

Lining the Bag

8 Cut two pieces of lining fabric each 10½in x 18in (26.7cm x 45.7cm). Join these together to make a tube (Fig 8). Press the seams open.

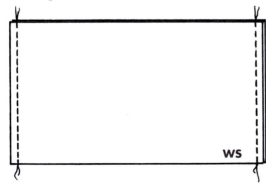

Fig 8

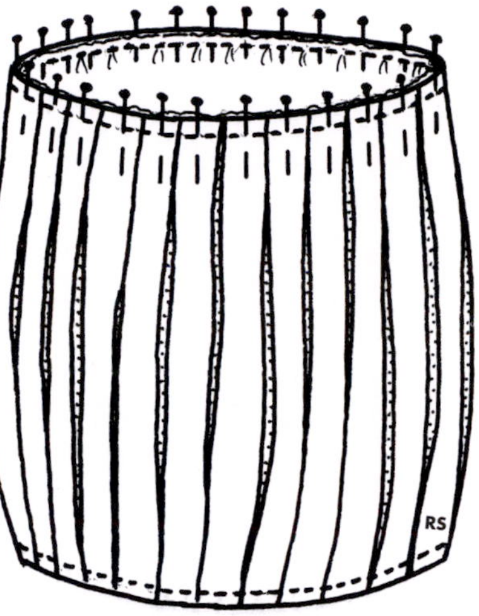

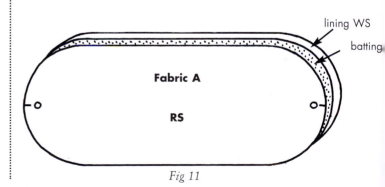

Fig 9

9 Use a long machine stitch to sew a gathering thread ¼in (6mm) from the top edge of the tube and another ¼in (6mm) from the bottom edge. Pull each thread up to gather the fabric until the gathered edges are both 24in (60.9cm). Distribute the gathers evenly. Place the lining inside the stitched bag, wrong sides facing. Line up the top and bottom edges of both bag and lining and pin together (Fig 9).

Making the Base of the Bag

10 The design drawn in Fig 10 on page 95 is half the base shape. Trace it on to a large piece of tracing paper, including the centre dotted line. Turn the tracing paper round and complete the base shape by tracing the other half, matching the centre dotted line. Mark the mid-points O on the tracing.

11 Use the traced base shape as a pattern to cut a base from fabric A, one from the lining fabric and one from wadding (batting). Place the three layers together with the two fabrics right sides facing *outwards* and the wadding (batting) sandwiched between them (Fig 11). Pin the layers together, matching the edges carefully. Tack (baste) around the shape through all layers about ¼in (6mm) from the edges. If desired, a cross-hatching of machine quilting can be stitched to strengthen the base of the bag (Fig 12).

Fig 11

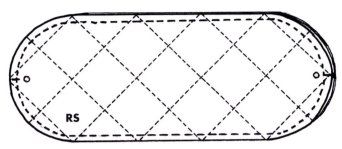

Fig 12

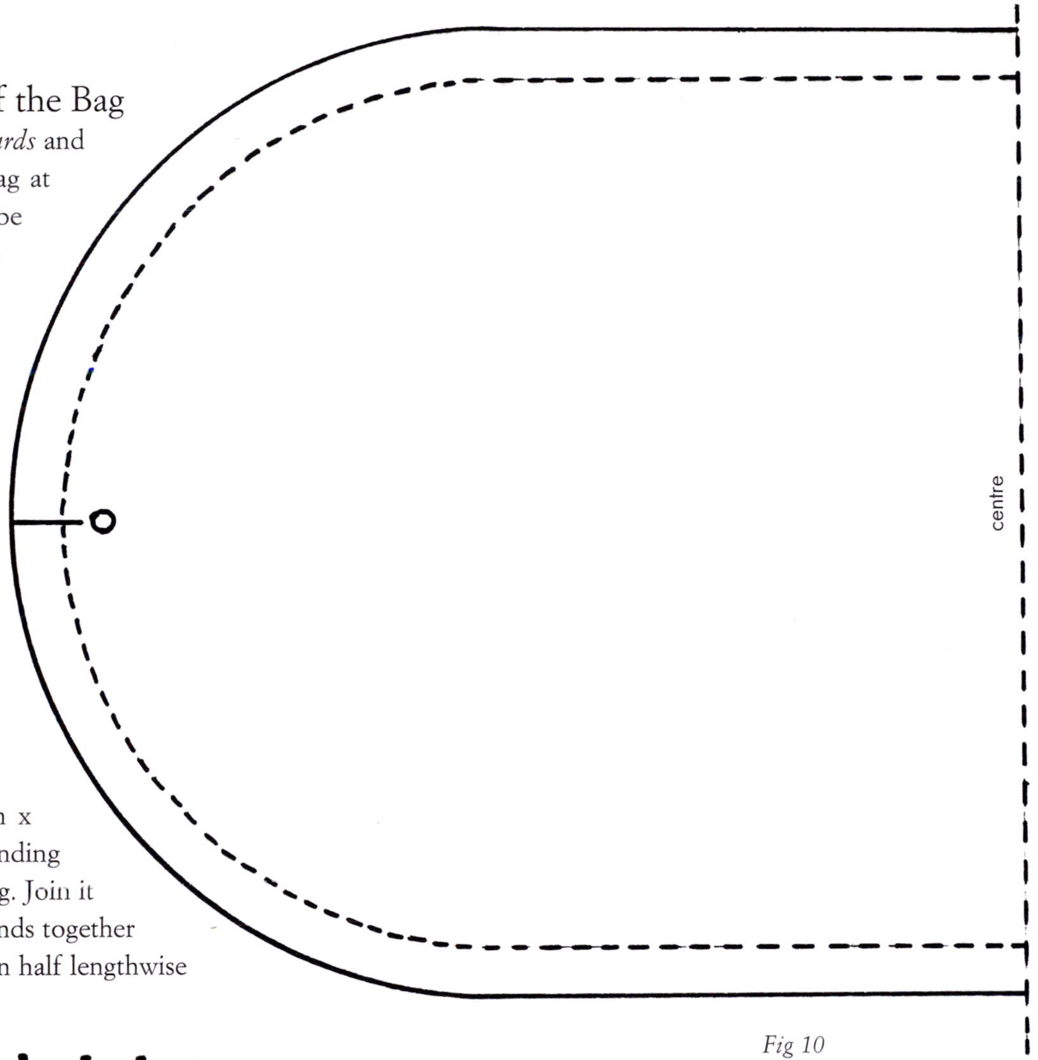

Assembling the Bottom of the Bag

12 Keep the bag right side *outwards* and hold it with the bottom of the bag at the top. The lining fabric should be inside the bag and fabric A on the outside. Place the layered base in position at the bottom end of the bag. The seam will finish up on the outside of the bag with bound edges, which gives a really firm base to the bag (see photograph on page 93). Match the mid-points O on the base with the seams in the bag lining. Pin the base to the bag, keeping all edges of fabric level (Fig 13). Stitch a ¼in (6mm) seam through all layers and then remove pins.

13 Cut a strip of fabric A 2½in x 24½in (6.3cm x 62.2cm) for the binding of the edges at the base of the bag. Join it into a loop by stitching the two ends together with a ¼in (6mm) seam. Fold it in half lengthwise with the right side *outwards*.

centre

Fig 10

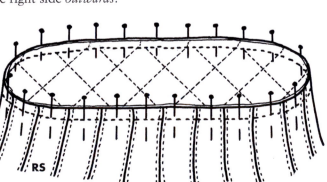

Fig 13

14 Pin the folded binding to the *outside* of the bottom of the bag, matching the raw edges of the binding with the raw edges of the bag (Fig 14). The folded loop of binding should just fit the base edges of the bag.

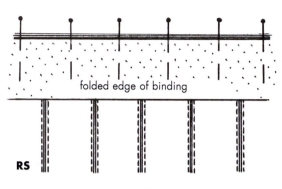

Fig 14

15 Stitch a ⅜in (8mm) seam through all the layers. Remove the pins and bring the folded edge of the binding over to the inside of the bag. Slipstitch the folded edge down by hand, just covering the line of machine stitches (Fig 15).

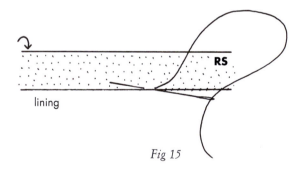

Fig 15

Making the Inner Drawstring Top

16 Cut two pieces of fabric, either fabric A or B or possibly another fabric altogether, each 6¼in x 13in (15.1cm x 33cm). Stitch the two shorter sides together with a ½in (12mm) seam, *not* the usual ¼in (6mm). Leave 2¼in (5.6cm) of each seam unstitched (Fig 16).

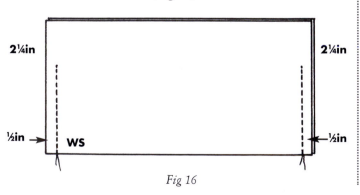

Fig 16

17 Finger-press the two seams open. Fold the raw edges of the seam allowances under to neaten them, including the unstitched sections. Stitch the folded edges (Fig 17).

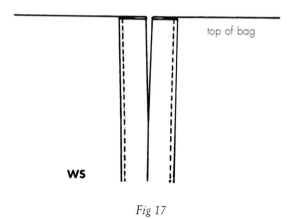

Fig 17

18 To make channels for the drawstring cords fold each of the two top edges over to the *wrong* side of the fabric and press a ¼in (6mm) turning. Fold again and press a ½in (12mm) turning and stitch close to the folded edge (Fig 18).

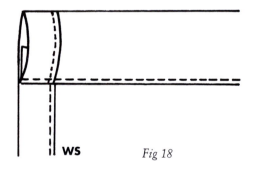

Fig 18

Making the Straps

19 From fabric B (or another fabric if you prefer) cut two strips, one 2½in x 40in (6.3cm x 101.5cm) and the other 2½in x 4½in (6.3cm x 11.3cm). Fold each strip in half lengthwise, right sides facing. Stitch one end and along the side of the long folded strip with the usual ¼in (6mm) seam, leaving the other end open (Fig 19). Trim the corners, turn the strip through to its right side and press. Stitch along the long side only of the short strip. Turn it through to its right side and press.

Fig 19

Assembling the Top of the Bag

20 As with the base of the bag, the seam allowances will be on the outside of the bag and are bound to give a firm top edge. Open the bag top and place the raw edge of the drawstring top section in it with its *wrong* side against the bag lining. Match the seams of the drawstring section with the seams in the lining. Pin the drawstring section to the top edges of the bag, matching the edges carefully.

21 At the same time pin the unstitched end of the long length of strap to the *outside* of the bag where one lining seam occurs. Thread the two D-rings on to the short length of strap. Fold it in half and pin both ends to the *outside* of the bag at the point where the other lining seam occurs (Fig 20). The edges of the straps should be level with the edges of the bag and the drawstring section. Stitch a ¼in (6mm) seam through all the layers, then remove the pins.

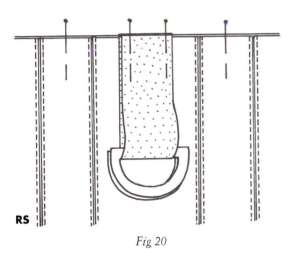

Fig 20

22 From fabric A cut a strip 2½in x 24½in (6.3cm x 62.2cm). This will be used to bind the top edges of the bag in the same way as the bottom edges were bound. Follow steps 13–15 to bind the top edges of the bag.

23 Cut two lengths of cord for the drawstrings, both 24in (60.9cm) long. Thread one cord through the two channels in the top of the bag, starting and finishing at the same side of the bag. Thread the other cord through, starting and finishing at the opposite side of the bag. Knot the ends of the cords or use beads to decorate the ends. Pulling both cords will close the bag.

Pauline Bugg's black and white drawstring bag uses strips of fabric in a Bargello-style arrangement to create a striking design. Alternating strips of contrasting fabrics could also be used effectively.

Smiley Suns and Stars Cot Quilt

This little cot quilt combines blanket stitch appliquéd suns with pieced stars. Sue FitzGerald made the quilt using my left-over blue and yellow fabrics. It uses two blue fabrics as backgrounds with a third as an outer background and border. A lighter effect could be achieved by using a yellow fabric instead of blue for the outer area of the quilt.

Finished size of block 7½in x 7½in (18.9cm x 18.9cm)

Finished size of quilt 36½in x 47in (92.7cm x 120.7cm)

Fabric Requirements

There are twelve sun blocks in the design using two yellow fabrics and six star blocks that use a different pair of yellow fabrics. If your fabric will not stretch to all twelve suns, use several similar fabrics to give a more scrappy look to the quilt.

Suns: 12in (30.4cm) of yellow fabric 42in (106.7cm) wide.

Sun faces: 4in (10cm) of a different yellow fabric 42in (106.7cm) wide.

Background for sun blocks: twelve squares of light blue fabric each cut 8in x 8in (20.2cm x 20.2cm).

First star fabric: 4in (10cm) of yellow fabric 42in (106.7cm) wide.

Second star fabric: 4in (10cm) of a different yellow fabric 42in (106.7cm) wide.

Background fabric for star blocks: 12in (30.4cm) of dark blue fabric 42in (106.7cm) wide.

Outer background and border: 30in (76cm) of fabric 42in (106.7cm) wide.

Backing: 38½in x 49in (97.8cm x 124.4cm).

Thicker thread: for the blanket stitch appliqué – I used Gütermann silk thread.

Iron-on fusible web: ¾yd (68.5cm) – I used Bondaweb, known in the USA as Wonder-Under.

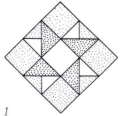

Fig 1

Construction

Making the Smiley Sun Blocks

From the chosen background fabric cut twelve squares each 8in x 8in (20.2cm x 20.2cm).

Blanket Stitch Appliqué

This technique uses a fusible web such as Bondaweb to stick down the raw edges of the appliqué pieces on to the background fabric before stitching around the design with blanket stitch. The Bondaweb is used to stick *only* the outer ⅛in (3mm) of each appliqué piece – this avoids the thick, stiff layers usually associated with fusible work. Be careful when using fusible web – see Tip on page 76.

1 Using the fusible web: Place the fusible web *smooth side uppermost* over the sun design shown in Fig 2 on page 100. Trace both the outer sun and the inner circle. Do not trace the sun's face at this stage. Mark the grain-line arrows on the tracing, keeping them at the very edge of the shapes rather than in the centre.

2 Cut out the traced sun shape roughly ¼in (6mm) beyond the outer drawn line as shown in Fig 3.

3 Carefully cut out the central area of fusible web and remove it, leaving only about ⅛in (3mm) remaining inside the drawn line (Fig 4).

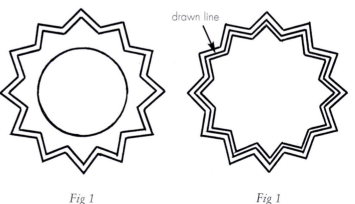

Fig 1   *Fig 1*

Use it all up!

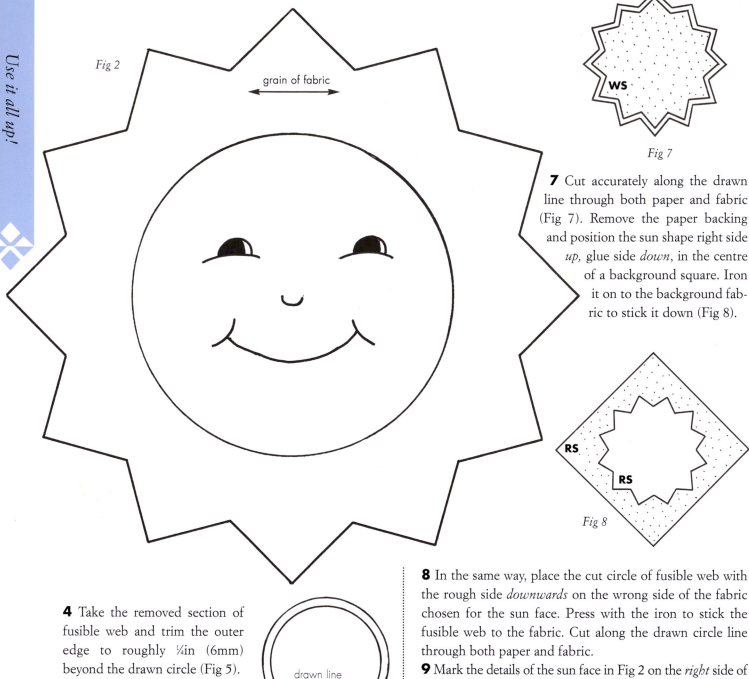

Fig 2

grain of fabric

WS

Fig 7

7 Cut accurately along the drawn line through both paper and fabric (Fig 7). Remove the paper backing and position the sun shape right side *up*, glue side *down*, in the centre of a background square. Iron it on to the background fabric to stick it down (Fig 8).

RS

RS

Fig 8

4 Take the removed section of fusible web and trim the outer edge to roughly ¼in (6mm) beyond the drawn circle (Fig 5).
5 Carefully cut out the central area of fusible web and remove it, leaving only about ⅛in (3mm) inside the drawn circle (Fig 6).
6 Place the outer spiky piece of fusible web with the rough side *downwards* on the *wrong* side of the fabric chosen for the sun, matching the grain-line arrow with the grain or weave of the fabric. Press with a hot iron to stick the fusible web to the fabric.

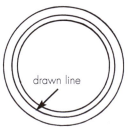

drawn line

Fig 5

drawn line

Fig 6

8 In the same way, place the cut circle of fusible web with the rough side *downwards* on the wrong side of the fabric chosen for the sun face. Press with the iron to stick the fusible web to the fabric. Cut along the drawn circle line through both paper and fabric.
9 Mark the details of the sun face in Fig 2 on the *right* side of the fabric circle by tracing the design using a sharp pencil, and a light box if necessary (see Tip). Match the grain or weave of the fabric with the grain-line arrow marked in Fig 2.

Tip
A light box for tracing designs on to fabric can be bought from business supply shops, but is expensive. All you really need is a flat, clear surface lit from below so that lines to be traced are highlighted through the fabric, such as a glass-topped table with a light beneath. If all else fails, tape the design to a window, tape the fabric over the top and trace the outline.

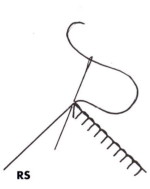

Fig 9

10 Remove the paper backing from the fabric circle. Position the circle right side up, glue side *down*, in the centre of the main sun shape (Fig 9). The circle can be turned to tilt the features slightly if desired so that each sun looks different from its neighbours. Sue FitzGerald aimed to set all her sun faces straight but one finished up slightly tilted, which we feel adds to the appeal. Iron the circle on to the main sun shape to stick it down.

11 Hand stitching the outline of the design: Use a slightly thicker thread than usual (I like the Gütermann silk thread) and a fine sewing needle like a Sharps 9 or 10. Black is often used to outline this type of design but any choice of colour will be fine. Stitch the outer rays first and then the circular sun face, using a blanket stitch. Try to keep the stitches all the same length, about ³⁄₁₆in (5mm) and evenly spaced (Fig 10). When turning sharp corners like the points of the sun rays, make one extra tiny stitch on the spot at the corner to keep that long corner stitch in place (Fig 11). Before stitching around the circular surface, the appliqué layers may be reduced by turning the whole piece over and cutting away the background area within the blanket stitched edges ¼in (6mm) away from the stitching. This is not obligatory, so if your nerve fails you, just leave the layers intact.

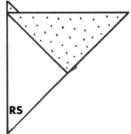

Fig 10

Fig 11

12 Stitching by machine: Many machines do an excellent blanket stitch, though you may need to practise stitching around corners and so on.

13 Stitching the sun face: Once the edges have been secured with blanket stitch use the thicker thread to embroider the details of the sun's face. Use backstitch or stem stitch for the lines and fill the eyes in with satin stitch.

14 Stick down and stitch all twelve smiley sun blocks in this way.

Making the Star Blocks

15 Six star blocks are needed for the quilt. For each block cut the following pieces:

Background fabric: four squares each 3in x 3in (7.5cm x 7.5cm);
One square 3¾in x 3¾in (9.4cm x 9.4cm) cut into four diagonally;
First star fabric: one square 3in x 3in (7.5cm x 7.5cm);
One square 3¾in x 3¾in (9.4cm x 9.4cm) cut into four diagonally;
Second star fabric: two squares 3⅜in x 3⅜in (8.4cm x 8.4cm) each cut in half diagonally.
Arrange the cut squares and triangles as in Fig 12 and check that you like the design.

16 To make the four pieced squares as in Fig 14, pin and stitch together one small triangle of blue background fabric and one small triangle of the first yellow fabric (Fig 13), using an exact ¼in (6mm) seam. Press the seam towards the blue triangle, ironing from the front. Stitch each set of two triangles in *exactly* the same arrangement as in Fig 13.

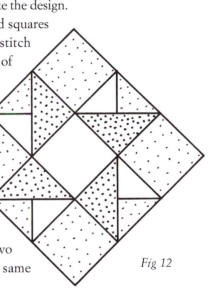

Fig 12

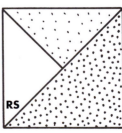

Fig 13

Fig 14

17 Pin and stitch together the two joined small triangles and a large triangle of the second yellow fabric (Fig 15). Press the seam towards the large triangle, ironing from the front. Trim the over-hanging corners back, level with the other edges of the fabric (Fig 16). Stitch together all four pieced squares in this way.

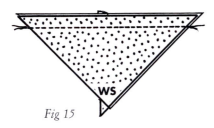

Fig 15

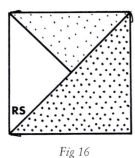

Fig 16

18 Arrange the four pieced stars and the five whole squares in the star design (Fig 17). Pin and stitch together the top row of three squares. Press seams away from the pieced square, ironing from the front.

19 Pin and stitch together the second row of three squares, pressing both seams in towards the centre square. Stitch together the third row of squares and press the seams out away from the pieced square as in row 1. This way the seams will lock together when the three rows are joined to make the nine-patch.

20 Stitch together the three rows, matching seams carefully. Press the seams to one side, ironing from the front. Stitch all six star blocks in this way.

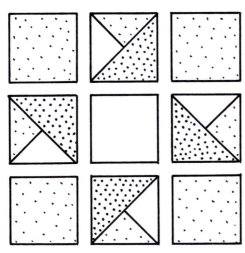

Fig 17

Assembling the Blocks

In addition to the eighteen blocks that are arranged on point, edging triangles are needed to fill in the gaps around the blocks. Cut these from one fabric, either blue as in Sue's quilt, or yellow to give a lighter effect. Ten larger triangles are needed for the side and the top and bottom edges, plus four smaller triangles for the corners of the quilt (Fig 18).

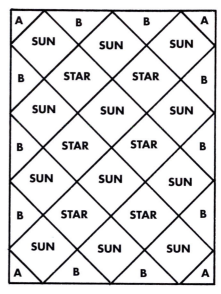

Fig 18

21 Cutting the small corner triangles (A): From the chosen outer background fabric cut two squares each 6½in x 6½in (15.8cm x 15.8cm). Cut each square in half diagonally (Fig 19).

Fig 19

22 Cutting the large edging triangles (B): If your fabric will allow, cut three squares from your outer background fabric each 12in x 12in (30.4cm x 30.4cm). Cut each square into four diagonally (Fig 20). Only ten of the large triangles are needed for the quilt. Do not use the remaining two for the corners as the grain of the fabric will be wrong.

Fig 20

Tip
If you are unable to cut three large 12in (30.4cm) squares from the fabric, draw the triangle shown in Fig 21 accurately on graph paper and stick it on to card to make a template. Use this template to draw around and cut out ten large triangles. Seam allowances are included. Be careful to match the grain-line arrow on the template with the fabric weave.

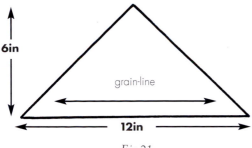

Fig 21

23 Arrange the blocks and edging triangles as in Fig 18. The design is pinned and stitched in diagonal rows as shown in Fig 22. Begin with row 1, pinning and stitching the three pieces together as in Fig 23. Press seams towards the sun block, ironing from the front.

24 Pin and stitch row 2 together, pressing seams towards the two sun blocks. Continue to pin and stitch rows 3, 4, 5 and 6 together, following Fig 22 for positioning the end triangles on each row. Press the seams towards the sun blocks each time, ironing from the front.

25 Stitch rows 1–6 together, row by row, matching seams carefully. Finally add the two corners to complete the design. Press the seams all in one direction, ironing from the front. If necessary trim the outer edges of the quilt to make them all level with each other.

Adding the Border

Sue's quilt has a border of the same outer background fabric cut 2½in (9.3cm) wide so that the blocks appear to float on this background. (See Bordering a Quilt page 117.)

Quilting

Sue quilted around the face and outer edge of each sun and also ¼in (6mm) within the edges of the blocks. The star blocks were quilted ¼in (6mm) away from the seams in the traditional way. A series of diagonal quilted lines in each of the outer edging triangles echoes the diagonal set of the sun and star blocks (for more ideas for quilting see page 122). The quilt is bound in the same dark blue fabric that was used as the background for the star blocks (see Finishing a Quilt page 117).

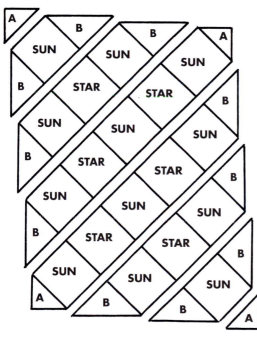

Fig 22

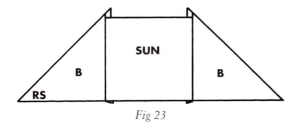

Fig 23

Crazy Quillow

The crazy scrap effect of the blocks in this quillow by Shirley Prescott is made by surrounding a central shape with three frames of fabric, using a different fabric for each centre and frame on the blocks. A foundation is used to keep the strips uniformly irregular (if that makes sense!) – this ensures that each block finishes up exactly the same size as the others. Twelve blocks are needed for the main quillow plus one extra block for the pillow section.

Finished size of Crazy block 9in x 9in (22.8cm x 22.8cm)

Finished size of quillow 55½in x 43½in (140.9cm x 110.5cm)

Fabric Requirements

Thirteen pieces of interesting fabric suitable for the centres of the blocks, approximately 5in x 5in (12.7cm x 12.7cm). These could be prints as in Shirley's quillow or even plain fabrics with numbers, letters of the alphabet or anything you fancy appliquéd on to them.

Scraps of assorted fabrics, as many as you have, for the strips around each block, plus the border of the cushion block, approximately 2½yd (2.28m) in total.

Sashing: ¾yd (68.5cm).

Outer border: ½yd (45.7cm).

Backing for quillow: a piece of fabric (or several pieces joined) 57in x 45in (144.7cm x 114.3cm).

Backing for cushion: (if possible same fabric as quilt backing): 20in x 20in (50.7cm x 50.7cm).

Working with a Foundation

Two types of foundation can be used for this work: one that is removed after the block has been completed, such as tracing paper, freezer paper or a woven tear-away foundation; or one that is left behind the block to give it stability like Vilene or calico. Using a permanent foundation does eliminate the tedious task of pulling all the paper from the block once it is finished but will make the block thicker and heavier, especially if calico is used. I prefer a fine Vilene which can be left in position without adding thickness and is also virtually transparent – a great help when piecing. Shirley used freezer paper, which she removed after the completion of each block.

Preparing for Sewing

To make it easier to stitch exactly on the drawn line on the foundation an open-front foot is needed for the machine so that you get a good view of both the line and the needle. The ¼in (6mm) foot for most machines does this job nicely, or you can cut away the centre part of a plastic foot. I used a hacksaw from a child's toolbox to do this with great success. Change the needle in your machine from the usual 80/12 to a larger 90/14 – this makes larger holes in the paper so that it can be removed more easily. The stitch length should be set even smaller than usual, approximately 18–20 stitches to 1in (2.5cm) for the same reason. Do a test run on a measured inch on some fabric and count the stitches so you will know the correct setting for your own machine. Just remember that you may have to unpick the odd line of stitches, so make sure that your stitches are not too small to make this possible.

Construction

1 Cut thirteen pieces of foundation such as tracing paper, freezer paper or a tear-away woven foundation, each 10in x 10in (25.3cm x 25.3cm). Use a ruler and sharp pencil to trace the complete design, including the numbers (given in Fig 1 in two halves actual size on pages 106 and 108) on to the foundation. Trace each half, matching up the dotted lines that mark the halfway line of the block to reproduce the entire design. The traced block should measure 9in x 9in (22.8cm x 22.8cm). Leave at least ¼in (6mm) beyond the drawn design on all sides of the foundation.

2 Make a template from the centre shape in Fig 2 on page 107. This is the exact shape of the centre of each block including the ¼in (6mm) seam allowance. If you are focusing on a specific design or motif on a piece of fabric it is helpful to cut the template from clear plastic.

3 Make one block at a time. Place the centre template on the *back* of the chosen fabric and draw around it. If your placement of the template is critical for the design you may

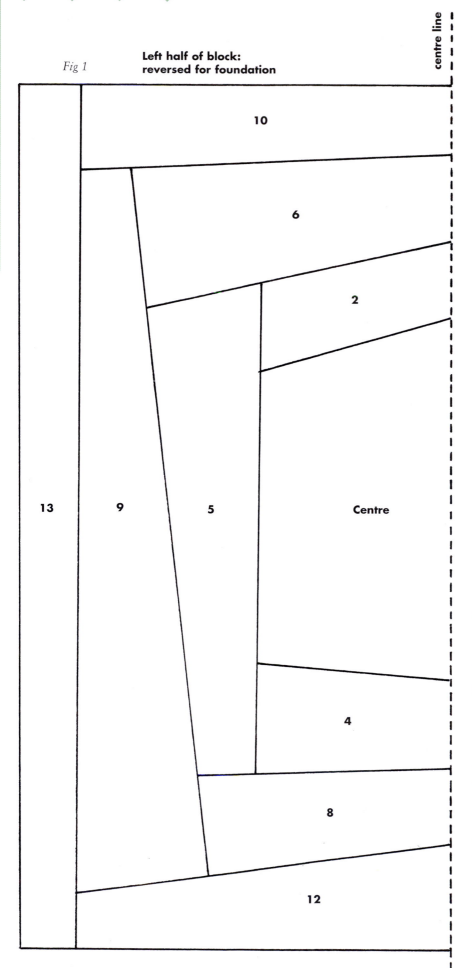

Fig 1

**Left half of block:
reversed for foundation**

centre line

10

6

2

13   9   5   Centre

4

8

12

have to place it on the *right* side of the fabric. If this is the case, turn the template over to its *reverse* side and draw around it. Cut out the drawn shape exactly on the line – the seam allowance is already included.

4 Place the cut centre right side *up* on the unmarked side of the foundation. The edges should extend ¼in (6mm) beyond the drawn centre shape. You can check this by viewing from the marked side of the foundation (Fig 3). If you cannot see too well through the foundation, hold it up against the light on the sewing machine. Pin the fabric in position. If you are using freezer paper you can press it in place by ironing from the marked side. Don't worry – the waxed coating on the unmarked side will not leave a deposit on the ironing board or the base of the iron.

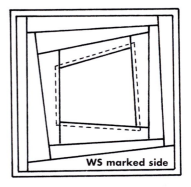

WS marked side

Fig 3

5 Select the three fabrics that will make the three frames of strips around the centre shape. From the first fabric cut four strips 1¾in (4.3cm) wide and 7in (17.7cm) long.

6 Place a cut strip with right side facing *outwards* on the unmarked side of the foundation over the area marked 2 on the foundation. Flip the strip over on to the centre shape with right sides facing and the edges matching (Fig 4). The strip will be longer than the centre shape but do not trim it down at this stage. Instead keep about the same amount of extra strip at each end of the centre shape as in Fig 4. Pin the strip in position and turn the whole thing over so that the marked side of the foundation is uppermost.

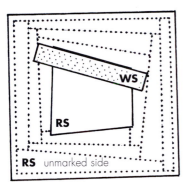

Fig 4

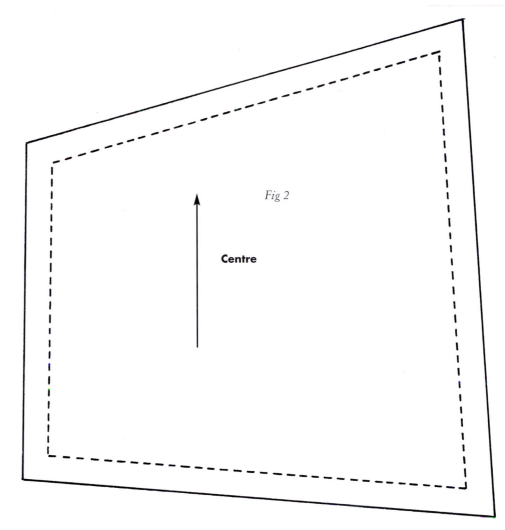

Centre

Fig 2

7 Stitch along the marked line between the centre and shape 2, extending two or three stitches beyond the beginning and end of the drawn line (Fig 5).

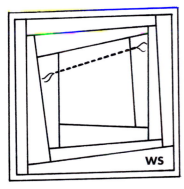

Fig 5

8 Turn to the right side (unmarked) and flip the strip over on to the foundation. Finger-press the seam and trim the strip at both ends to about ¼in (6mm) beyond shape 2 (Fig 6). Press the strip into place, ironing from the front.
9 Repeat this with a 7in (17.7cm) strip of the same fabric on shape 3, then shape 4 and finally shape 5 to complete the frame around the centre shape (Fig 7).

10 From the fabric chosen for the second frame around the block cut three strips 2in x 7in (5cm x 17.7cm) plus one strip 2in x 8in (5cm x 20.2cm). This frame of strips will be easier to position if the stitched strips are trimmed down at this stage. Turn the foundation to the marked side and place a thin ruler along the stitching line between shape 2 and shape 6. Pull the foundation back along this line against the edge of the ruler. Don't worry if the foundation pulls away from the stitches at the ends of the seams. Trim the fabric by eye or using a ruler and cutter to a ¼in (6mm) beyond the folded edge of the foundation (Fig 8).

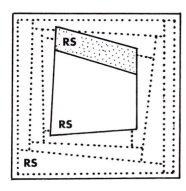

Fig 6

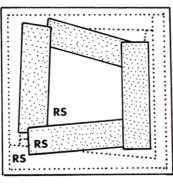

Fig 7

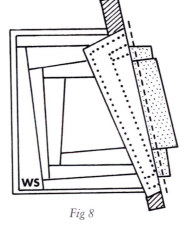

Fig 8

Use it all up!

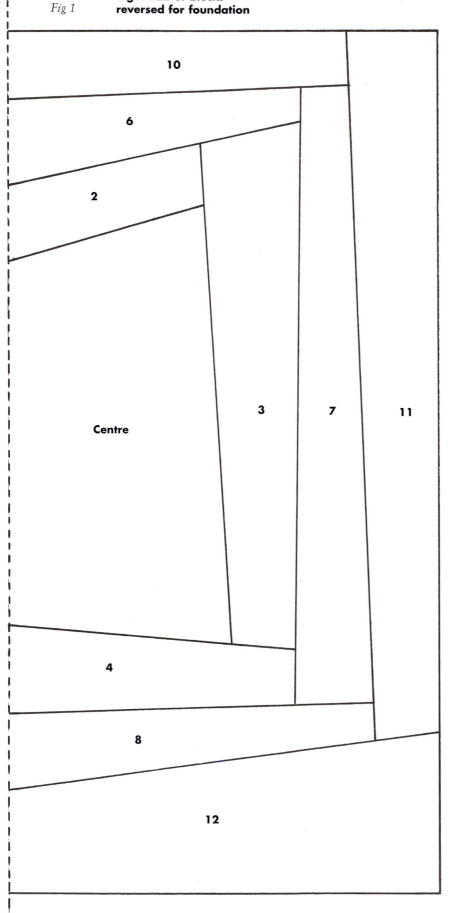

Fig 1

**Right half of block:
reversed for foundation**

10

6

2

Centre

3   7   11

4

8

12

11 In the same way trim the fabric strip down to ¼in (6mm) beyond the line between shape 3 and shape 7, then the line between shape 4 and 8 and finally the line between shape 5 and 9.

12 Turn the block back to the front. Take one of the 7in (17.7cm) strips of the second fabric and position it on strip 2 with right sides facing, lining up the long edges. The top strip will be longer than strip 2 so keep about the same amount of extra strip overhanging at each end of strip 2 (Fig 9). Pin in position and turn the foundation over to the marked side.

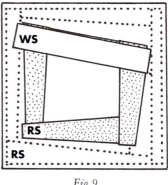

Fig 9

13 Stitch along the drawn line between shape 2 and shape 6 through both layers of fabric, sewing two or three stitches beyond the drawn line at the start and finish. Turn to the right side and flip the fabric over on to the foundation. Trim the strip at both ends to about ¼in (6mm) beyond shape 6. Press into position with an iron (Fig 10).

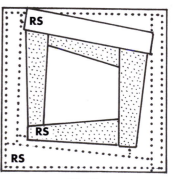

Fig 10

14 Repeat this with 7in (17.7cm) strips on sides 7 and 8 and using the 8in (20.2cm) strip on side 9. Press all four strips into place on the foundation.

15 Use a ruler placed on the lines between this round of strips and the next round to trim the fabric down as before.

16 From the fabric chosen for the final frame of the block cut two strips 1¾in x 8½in (4.3cm x 21.5cm) for sides 10 and 11, one strip 2½in x 9½in (6.3cm x 24.1cm) for side 12 and one strip 1½in x 10in (3.7cm x 25.3cm) for side 13.

17 Pin and stitch on the fabric strips for sides 10, 11, 12 and 13. Press the strips into place on the foundation.

18 Trim the block and foundation to exactly ¼in (6mm) beyond the outer drawn line (Fig 11). This makes a block 9½in x 9½in (24.1cm x 24.1cm). It is a good idea to leave the foundation in place until all the blocks are joined with sashing as it adds stability and the stitching line is marked ready for use.

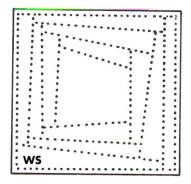

Fig 11

19 Following the same method, make the remaining twelve Crazy blocks. Twelve will be used for the quillow and the remaining one for the cushion front.

Adding Sashing Strips

1 From the sashing fabric cut the following:
Eight strips 3in x 9½in (7.5cm x 24.1cm);
Three strips 3in x 32½in (7.5cm x 82.4cm);
Two strips 3in x 44in (7.5cm x 111.7cm);
Two strips 3in x 37½in (7.5cm x 95.2cm).

2 Arrange twelve blocks in four rows of three blocks. Pin and stitch a short strip of sashing between the blocks in each row (Fig 12), a total of eight strips. Press the seams towards the sashing, ironing from the front.

3 Pin and stitch three strips each 3in x 32½in (7.5cm x 82.4cm) between the four rows of blocks (Fig 13). Press the seams towards the sashing, ironing from the front.

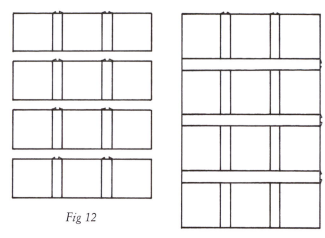

Fig 12

Fig 13

4 Pin and stitch the two side strips, each 3in x 44in (7.5cm x 111.7cm) to the sides of the quilt, pressing seams outwards away from the quilt.

5 Pin and stitch the top and bottom strips each 3in x 37½in (7.5cm x 95.2cm) to the quilt, pressing seams outwards (Fig 14). You can remove the foundation now.

6 From the fabric chosen for the outer border cut two strips 3¼in x 49in (8.2cm x 124.2cm) and two 3¼in x 43in (8.2cm x 109.2cm). Pin and stitch the two side strips to the quilt, pressing seams outwards. Pin and stitch the top and bottom strips to the quilt, pressing seams outwards (Fig 15).

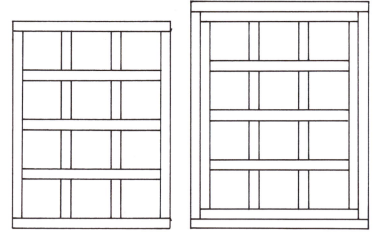

Fig 14

Fig 15

Quilting

Layer the quilt with wadding (batting) and backing fabric, each cut about 1in (2.5cm) larger than the quilt on all sides 57in x 45in (144.7cm x 114.3cm). Safety-pin or tack (baste) the layers together. Shirley Prescott quilted her quillow by machine in the ditch or seamline of each frame around each centre shape and also in the seam between the sashing and the outer border. For more ideas for quilting see page 122.

Constructing the Cushion Pocket

1 To the remaining Crazy block add a border frame from a suitable fabric. For this cut two strips 2in x 9½in (5cm x 24.1cm) and two strips 2in x 12½in (5cm x 31.7cm). Pin and stitch the two shorter strips to the sides of the block, pressing seams outwards. Pin and stitch the two longer strips to the top and bottom of the block, pressing seams outwards. Now remove the foundation.

2 Use the left-over fabrics from the block to cut strips each 1½in x 4in (3.7cm x 10.1cm). Stitch these together to make four bands each 4in x 12½in (10.1cm x 31.7cm) (Fig 16). You should need twelve strips for each band.

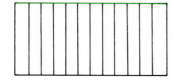

Fig 16

3 Pin and stitch two bands to either side of the cushion block. Press seams outwards, away from the block.

4 From the fabric used to frame the Crazy block (or another if you have run out) cut four squares each 4in x 4in (10.1cm x 10.1cm). Pin and stitch these to either end of the remaining two bands of strips, pressing seams towards the bands (Fig 17).

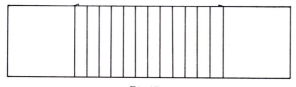

Fig 17

5 Pin and stitch these bands to the top and bottom of the cushion block, matching seams carefully. Press seams outwards, away from the block (Fig 18).

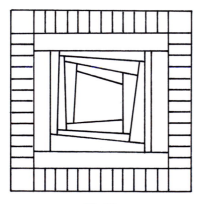

Fig 18

6 Cut a piece of wadding (batting) and a piece of backing fabric, if possible using the same fabric as the quilt back, about ½in (12mm) larger on all sides than the pieced top. Place the wadding (batting) on a flat surface and position the backing fabric on it, right side up. Place the pieced top right side *down* on to it. Pin and stitch a ¼in (6mm) seam around three sides of the block, leaving the top side open (Fig 19).

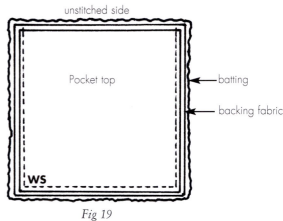

Fig 19

7 Trim away the extra wadding (batting) and backing fabric. Turn the pocket right side out, pushing the corners out carefully without damaging the stitching.

8 Pin or tack (baste) the layers together and quilt the block. Shirley quilted by machine in the ditch between each frame of the Crazy block and between the last frame and the pieced border.

Assembling the Quillow

1 Place the quilt right side *down* on a flat surface and position the pocket centrally at the top end with its right side *down* and the raw edges lined up with the edges of the quilt. Tack (baste) these edges together ready for binding (Fig 20).

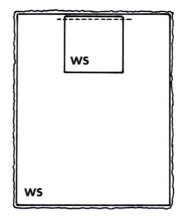

2 Bind the two sides of the quilt, following the instructions on page 124. Shirley used 8in (20.3cm) lengths of left-over fabrics joined together for her binding. Next bind the bottom edge and finally the top edges, including the raw edges of both quilt and pocket.

Fig 20

3 Pin and carefully hand stitch the two sides of the cushion in place on the quilt. The bottom side is left open for storing the quilt. The side seams take a lot of strain but must be hand-stitched as any machine-stitching would spoil the front of the quilt. To add strength, stitch into the wadding (batting) and sew each side twice. Reinforce the corners with extra stitches, and if you can, stitch right through without your stitches showing – this will strengthen the corners even more.

Folding the Quillow

Place the quilt right side up on a flat surface. Fold the sides of the quilt over in line with the edges of the pocket (Fig 21a). Pull the pocket through to its right side, enclosing the top two folded sides of the quilt (Fig 21b). Now fold the quilt over so that the bottom edges meet the open end of the pocket (Fig 21c). Finally, bring the folded edge up into the pocket so that all the quilt is inside (Fig 21d).

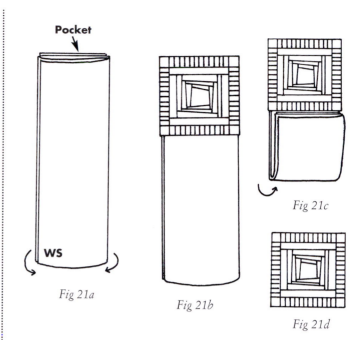

Fig 21a

Fig 21b

Fig 21c

Fig 21d

The quillow is folded and neatly contained in the pocket to create a crazy cushion.

'I Spy' Scrap Quilt

This small quilt was made by Kate Riddleston for her grandson Jacob. She collected pieces of fabric that showed different objects, animals, toys – anything that could be easily identified and talked about with a small child. These were all cut into 3½in (8.8cm) squares and bordered before being joined together to make the quilt. Photographs of Jacob's mother and father transferred on to fabric were also included, plus the letters of the alphabet that made up his name and the seven colours of the rainbow. In the bottom right-hand corner of the quilt is a photograph of the doting grandmother herself. Instead of layering the quilt with wadding (batting) and a backing fabric, Kate used polyester fleece in a rich blue to back the quilt. She tied the quilt at regular intervals to keep the layers in place and bound the edges with toning blue fabric. Using fleece gave a really cuddly feel to the piece – ideal for children's quilts or quillows.

Finished size of 'I Spy' block 3in x 3in (7.5cm x 7.5cm)

Finished size of quilt 58in x 59in (147.2 cm x 149.7cm)

Fabric Requirements

137 pictures: all different, each cut 3½in x 3½in (8.8cm x 8.8cm).

Sashing fabric for blocks: 1½yd (1.37m). If there isn't enough sashing fabric available try making the horizontal sashing strips from one fabric and the long vertical strips from another.

Red dividing strips: 10in (25.3cm) of 44in (111cm) wide fabric.

Blue surrounding border: ½yd (45.6cm).

Fleece for combined wadding (batting) and backing: 60in x 61in (152.3cm x 154.8cm).

Binding: 16in (40.6cm) of 44in (111cm) wide fabric.

Fig 1

Construction

1 Collect 137 different pictures on fabric, including if possible animals, vehicles, letters, numbers, colours and so on. Trade them with other quilters to add to your collection. If you cut a 3½in (8.8cm) square from template plastic it can be positioned on the front of the fabric to capture the best possible piece of the fabric. Draw around the template and cut out exactly on the drawn line.

2 Kate stitched a narrow frame around each 'I Spy' square before arranging and stitching them together. It is quicker and easier to arrange the squares in rows first and then add the sashing strips to join them together. Arrange the squares in eleven vertical rows as in Fig 1. There are twelve squares in each of the six shorter rows and thirteen in each of the

five longer rows. Leave gaps between each square and each row for the sashing and the red strips.

3 From the chosen sashing fabric cut a strip 1½in (3.7cm) wide – cut parallel to the selvage to be less stretchy. From this strip cut eleven pieces each 1½in x 3½in (3.7cm x 8.8cm). Place these between the twelve squares of the first vertical row of pictures (Fig 2).

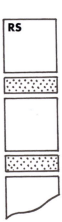

Fig 2

4 Pin and stitch each sashing strip to the blocks, joining together into one long strip (Fig 3).

5 From a 1½in (3.7cm) cut strip of sashing fabric cut twelve pieces each 1½in x 3½in (3.7cm x 8.8cm). Pin and stitch these between the thirteen squares to join row 2 together.

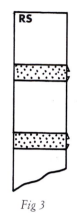

Fig 3

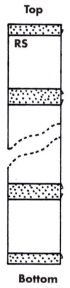

Top

Bottom

Fig 5

6 Continue to cut pieces of sashing fabric 1½in x 3½in (3.7cm x 8.8cm), pinning and stitching them between the squares of each vertical row until all eleven rows are joined (Fig 4). There should be six rows with twelve squares (A) and five rows with thirteen squares (B). Press all seams towards the sashing strips, ironing from the front.

7 From the sashing fabric cut twenty-two strips each 1in x 3½in (2.5cm x 8.8cm). Add one strip to the top and bottom of each joined row of squares (Fig 5). Press seams towards the sashing, ironing from the front.

Joining the Rows

8 From the sashing fabric cut twelve strips each 1in x 48½in (2.5cm x 123.2cm), pinning and stitching these to each side of the six shorter rows of twelve squares (Fig 6). Press the seams towards the sashing strips, ironing from the front.

9 From the sashing fabric cut ten strips each 1in x 52½in (2.5cm x 133.3cm), pining and stitching these to each side of the five longer rows of thirteen squares. Press the seams towards the sashing strips.

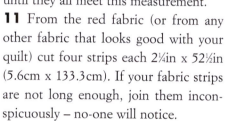

Fig 4

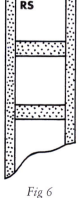

Fig 6

10 From the blue border fabric (or from any other fabric that looks good with your quilt) cut twelve strips, each 2½in x 4½in (6.2cm x 11.3cm). Stitch one strip to the top and bottom of each of the six shorter, twelve-square rows (Fig 7). Each row of joined squares should measure 52½in (133.3cm). If any do not, try stretching out the row with a steam iron or re-stitching some seams until they all meet this measurement.

11 From the red fabric (or from any other fabric that looks good with your quilt) cut four strips each 2¼in x 52½in (5.6cm x 133.3cm). If your fabric strips are not long enough, join them inconspicuously – no-one will notice.

12 Arrange the eleven rows of 'I Spy' squares with the four red strips as in Fig 8, then stitch the rows together. Press seams towards the sashing, ironing from the front.

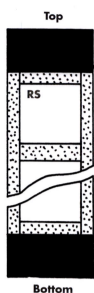

Top

Bottom

Fig 7

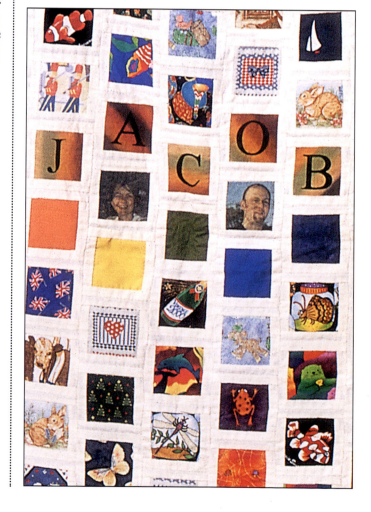

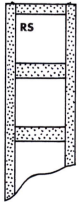

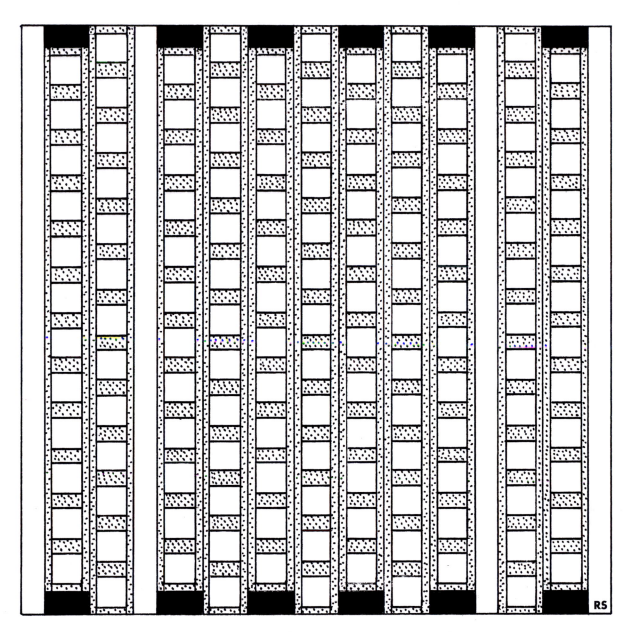

Fig 8

Adding the Borders

Cut two strips from your chosen outer border fabric each 3½in x 52½in (8.8cm x 133.3cm). Pin and stitch them to either side of the quilt. Press seams outwards, away from the quilt. Now cut two strips from the border fabric each 3½in x 57½in (8.8cm x 146cm). Pin and stitch them to the top and bottom of the quilt. Press seams outwards, away from the quilt. (See Bordering a Quilt page 117.)

Layering and Tying the Quilt

Place the quilt right side *upwards* on to the *wrong* side of the piece of fleece. Pin the two layers together at regular intervals about 3in–4in (7.5cm–10cm) apart, ready for tying. For details of tying see page 122. To finish, Kate used blue fabric that matched the border fabric to bind her quilt. For details on finishing and binding a quilt, see pages 117 and 122.

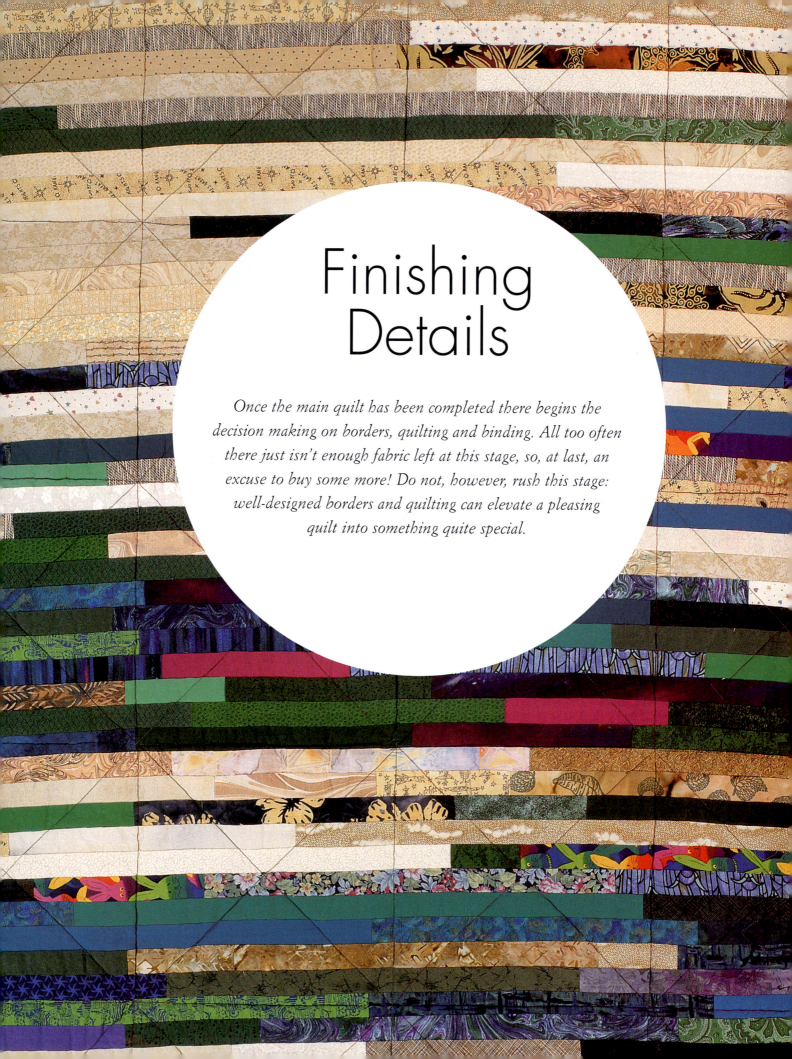

Finishing
Details

Once the main quilt has been completed there begins the decision making on borders, quilting and binding. All too often there just isn't enough fabric left at this stage, so, at last, an excuse to buy some more! Do not, however, rush this stage: well-designed borders and quilting can elevate a pleasing quilt into something quite special.

Finishing a Quilt

This final section provides general information on finishing your quilt and includes how to make borders, back your quilt and bind the edges. There are also some ideas on quilting.

Bordering a Quilt

The borders used on the quilts throughout the book have been described in the projects. Here, I give some general advice on bordering a quilt. Hopefully you found the borders shown on each project quilt appealing, but there may be a problem with having enough fabric left over to make them. Some scrap quilts look best without any extra border at all, like Pat Mitchell's quilt on page 11, which just has a wide binding. Others are so busy that they just need one or two simple frames around them. If your fabric will not stretch to this, let the borders wait until you have found a new fabric that will frame the quilt well and then use that. It doesn't matter if a fabric has not been used in the quilt as long as it looks as though it belongs. A 3in–4in (7.5cm–10cm) border for a bed quilt can be cut from 1yd (91.3cm) of fabric, although 1½yd (1.37m) would give a wider border with just one central join on each side. You can get away with several joins in a border strip provided they are placed at regular intervals so that they look planned.

Adding Framing Borders

1 Lay the quilt top on a flat surface and measure its length down the *centre*, not the edge. If you always do this and cut the borders to match the centre measurements there is less danger of the quilt edges spreading to give wavy borders.

2 Cut two strips of border fabric in the chosen width and a length to match the quilt measurement – for the side borders. Pin and stitch each side strip to the quilt, easing in any fullness in the quilt as you pin. Work on a flat surface and match the centres and both ends before pinning the rest. Press the seams outwards, away from the quilt (Fig 1).

3 Measure the quilt plus side borders from side to side across the centre. Cut two strips of border fabric in the chosen width and a length to match this measurement. Pin and stitch these to the top and bottom of the quilt, matching centres and both ends (Fig 2). Press seams outwards from the quilt. If another border is planned, measure the quilt down its centre again and repeat the process, sides first and then top and bottom.

4 You may prefer to make your border with cornerstones, that is, a square of different fabric in each corner of the border (Fig 3). Measure the quilt across its centre in *both*

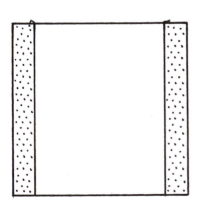

Fig 1

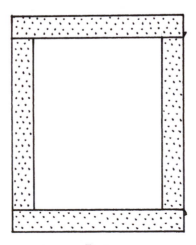

Fig 2

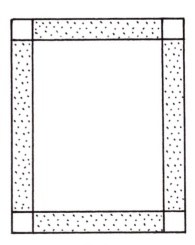

Fig 3

directions and cut strips of the border fabric in your chosen width and in lengths to match these measurements. Stitch the side strips to the quilt as usual, pressing the seams outwards away from the quilt. Cut four squares of fabric for the cornerstones the same size as the cut width of the border strips. Stitch one of these to either end of both top and bottom border strips (Fig 4). Press the seams towards the long strip. Pin and stitch these border strips to the top and bottom of the quilt, matching seams carefully (Fig 5). Press the seams outwards, away from the quilt. If a second border with cornerstones is planned, re-measure the quilt after the first border is added and repeat the process (Fig 6).

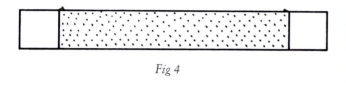

Fig 4

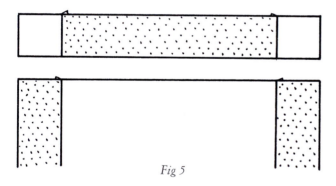

Fig 5

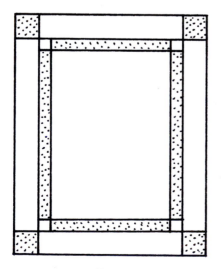

Fig 6

Pieced Borders

Having framed your quilt with one fabric, you may decide it needs a pieced border next. One option is to echo an element of the main quilt design in the pieced border. In Julia Reed's Daisy Chain quilt on page 83 she uses small squares to make a rich multi-fabric border that echoes the diagonal chain of squares in the main quilt. A pieced border gives the chance to really use up the left-overs, even if they have to be supplemented with extra new fabrics. As long as the colours tone with the quilt, pieces of fabric scrounged from quilter friends to add to your own will fit in surprisingly well.

Borders that use a specific repeated design like the triangles around my Magic Lanterns quilt on page 35 can be a problem, as it is not always possible to make repeat designs for border strips in an exact measurement to fit the quilt. The Flying Geese border in Victoria Gladwin's scrap sampler quilt (right) is another example of this. In both cases the same strategy was used. The border strips were pieced first, slightly longer than the sides of the quilt then extra framing strips were added all around the quilt to bring it up to the correct size to fit the borders. The Magic Lanterns quilt had two frames added before the pieced border (see below). Victoria's quilt needed extra strips added just to the top and bottom before the Flying Geese borders would fit nicely. She then echoed this strip in the final border of the quilt.

The border for Victoria Gladwin's quilt echoes the scrap fabric theme of the blocks, with extra spacing strips top and bottom so that the Flying Geese border fits neatly around the quilt.

'I love checks, stripes and rustic colours and enjoyed combining them in my sampler quilt. It's the first quilt I have made that I still love after it is finished.' **Victoria Gladwin**

Backing a Quilt

Finding five to seven yards or metres of fabric for the back of a quilt is another good way of using up your stored yardage. It is quite possible to combine several fabrics in a quilt back which can also create extra interest. If you have a piece of something special that you just cannot bear to cut up, use it as the central panel of the quilt back and build out from it with strips of other complementary fabrics (Fig 1). Make the piecing as simple as possible since it is more difficult to match exactly the front and back designs if the back is too complex.

A simple series of wide vertical strips in different fabrics can be very pleasing (Fig 2). If the fabric lengths are insufficient for this, add horizontal strips at the top and bottom (Fig 3). Should you hanker to combine the quilt left-

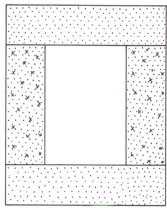

Fig 1

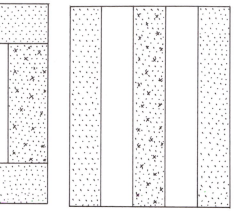

Fig 2

Jenny Lyons used left-over strips from her scrap Pineapple quilt (page 23) for the centre panel featured on the back of her quilt.

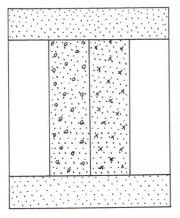

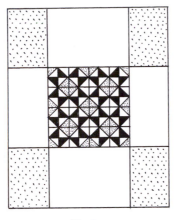

Fig 3   *Fig 4*

overs in an intricate pieced design for the back, limit this to the centre area and surround it with wide strips or pieces of other fabrics (Fig 4). If the back shifts a little during quilting and finishes up not quite square against the front of the quilt, this is far more noticeable when there are narrow border strips around the edges of the quilt back.

Don't agonize that the quilting done from the front of the quilt will not relate to the piecing on the back. It is surprising how compatible they seem when you turn the quilt over and have a look. Just take extra care when putting the layers together to centre both front and back sections as accurately as possible.

Large pieces of flannel were joined for the back of Janet Covell's Strip Snowball quilt (page 44).

Ideas for Quilting

When the quilt top is completed and layered with wadding (batting) and backing, the next consideration is how to quilt it. I am not concerned here with the various techniques of quilting – there are plenty of books that deal with this aspect. What I am suggesting is that you find a way of quilting the project that gives you the most satisfaction.

The first question is – do you *like* quilting? Do you enjoy quilting by hand or by machine? If you need to get it done quickly, a simple grid of machine quilting might be best. If you crave hand work that is always there to be picked up at odd moments, it is worth the laborious tacking (basting) of the quilt layers ready for weeks or even months of satisfying activity.

Consider the person for whom the quilt is being made: are they worth months of hand quilting? Do they need an heirloom or will they then be too intimidated to use the quilt at all? I am not being unkind or judgemental, just realistic!

If you need more practice at quilting, especially machine quilting, a small scrap quilt made for someone who will love using it but knows nothing about sewing is the perfect project. Just restrain yourself from pointing out all the faults when they admire it: they will never notice unless you insist upon showing them.

Remember that you are allowed to combine hand and machine quilting. I find basting a large quilt very tedious and do not have the space to do it efficiently at home, so will often safety-pin the layers thoroughly and begin with a skeleton design of machine quilting using a walking foot to keep everything in place. Then I add more intricate quilting by hand, removing the safety-pins where necessary to accommodate my quilting hoop. Some day soon I am going to start filling up areas with free machine quilting, using some of those wonderful variegated threads that look so exciting. These first efforts will definitely be used on projects for non-critical small children so I can improve my techniques while still making real quilts, not just practice pieces.

You might feel that some projects will look better without any obvious quilting and prefer to tie the layers together, as Kate Riddleston did on her 'I-Spy' quilt. I have given detailed instructions for this technique below as it is not always covered in general quilting books.

If you really do not enjoy quilting at all or do not have the time, there is always the option of getting the quilt professionally quilted with a long-arm machine. My Corner Log Cabin quilt on page 17 was quilted in this way by Jenny Spencer from Mildenhall in Suffolk. I was really pleased with the finished design and enjoyed seeing some one else's ideas used on my quilt. I felt no guilt about not doing everything myself. I love quilting but like most quilters have too many ideas and not enough time to make them all. If you want to use someone else's talents to complete a project, find a professional quilter whose work you admire and enjoy her expertise.

Enjoyment is definitely the word here. If quilting is not a pleasure for you, explore the alternatives and keep the dutiful aspects to a minimum. If, like me, you love it, have one quilting project constantly available so that it is always there to soothe and give solace (the hand quilting) or to excite and stimulate (the machine quilting).

Knotting or Tying a Quilt

Tying the layers of a quilt together with small knots is an efficient way of holding everything in place, either instead of quilting or alongside the quilting in areas like seam junctions where an extra holding-down action is needed. I have always made a double reef knot (thanks to my Girl Guide training!) but recently have discovered a slip knot used apparently in Amish quilts which is quick, easy and really secure.

1 Mark the position of each knot to be made with a glass-headed pin. If you remove the pins one by one as you make each knot you will know which ones still need to be processed. Knots can be made either on the front of the quilt as part of the design or on the back. For really discreet knotting, work from the back of the quilt using thread that matches the front, changing the thread colour where necessary. The small bar stitch on the quilt front will be scarcely noticeable. Knots need to be a maximum of 3in–4in (7.5cm–10cm) apart if they are the only method of holding the layers of the quilt together.

2 To make a knot, use a double thickness of normal sewing thread, or thicker embroidery thread if you prefer. Quilting thread is not suitable as it is waxed and is too springy to hold the knot securely. Working from whichever side of the quilt that the knots will be made, push the needle straight through all the layers of the quilt. Pull the needle through, leaving about 2in (5cm) of thread on the surface of the quilt. Bring the needle straight back up through the quilt about ⅛in–¼in (3mm–6mm) away from the point where it came through (Fig 1).

3 Hold the 2in (5cm) length of thread straight. Take the needle behind it to the left, then across the front to the right

(Fig 2). Bring the needle up through the loop to form a slip knot (Fig 3). Now pull the needle until the knot begins to tighten (Fig 4).

4 Finally, pull both ends of the thread to tighten the knot. Trim both threads to about ⅜in (4cm–5cm) or leave them longer for a more decorative effect.

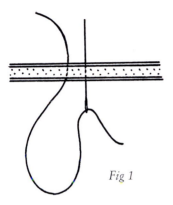

Fig 1

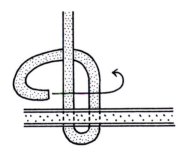

Fig 2

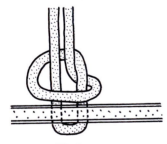

Fig 3

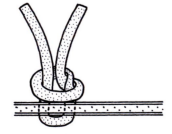

Fig 4

Binding a Quilt

Here I describe two methods for binding a quilt; one that uses four strips of binding with squared corners, which is suitable for designs with a horizontal and vertical emphasis such as sashed quilts, and one that uses continuous binding with mitred corners.

Before adding the final binding, check that the quilt lies flat and the corners are really square. Tacking (basting) with small stitches near to the edge of the quilt will help keep it flat and avoid wavy edges. Trim the wadding (batting) and backing fabric down to a scant ¼in (6mm) beyond the quilt top (Fig 1).

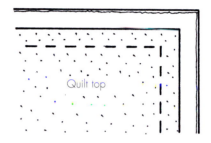

Quilt top

Fig 1

It is quite likely that the strips for the binding will have to be joined to make the lengths needed for the quilt. You may even want to add to the overall design with a multi-fabric binding where many short lengths have been joined. The binding will lie flatter and be easier to handle if the joins are made on the bias, making a 45° angle with the long edges of the strip. When stitching the binding to the quilt use a walking foot on your machine so that all the layers are fed through the machine evenly.

Joining the Strips

Cut all strips for the binding 2½in (6.3cm) wide. Trim the ends of each strip at an angle of 45° as in Fig 2. To do this, position the 45° mark on a rotary ruler along the top of the strip and cut along the ruler's edge (Fig 3 overleaf).

To join the strips, place two strips as in Fig 4 (overleaf) with right sides facing. Stitch a ¼in (6mm) seam as shown and then press the diagonal seam open.

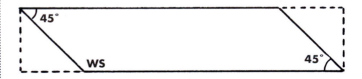

45°   WS   45°

Fig 2

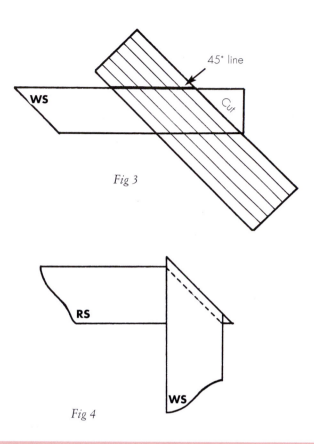

Fig 3

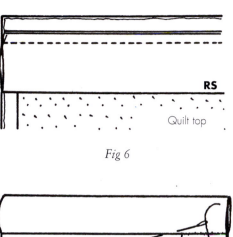

Fig 6

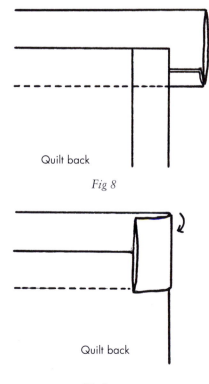

Fig 7

4 Pin and stitch the folded binding to the top and bottom of the quilt in the same way, leaving about ¾in (1.9cm) of binding extending beyond the quilt at each end (Fig 8). Trim this back to about ½in (12mm) and fold in over the quilt edge (Fig 9). Fold the binding over to the back of the quilt and slipstitch in place (Fig 10), making sure that the corners are really square before you stitch them.

Fig 4

Square-cornered Binding

1 Cut four strips of fabric for the binding, each 2½in (6.3cm) wide. The two side strips should measure the length of the quilt from top to bottom. The two strips for the top and bottom edges should measure the width of the quilt from side to side plus 1½in (3.8cm). Shorter lengths can be joined if you do not have enough fabric.

2 Take each side binding strip and fold it in half, right side *outwards*, without pressing. Pin a folded strip to one side of the quilt, matching the edges of the binding with the edge of the quilt top (Fig 5). Stitch a seam ¼in (6mm) from the edge of the quilt top through all the layers (Fig 6). Repeat this with the second strip on the other side of the quilt.

3 Bring the folded edge of the binding over to the back and stitch in place by hand, just covering the line of machine stitches (Fig 7).

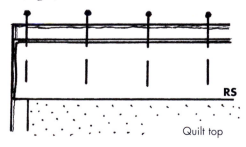

Fig 5

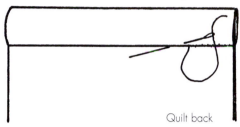

Quilt back

Fig 8

Quilt back

Fig 9

Quilt back

Fig 10

Continuous Binding with Mitred Corners

1 Make a length of binding strip 2½in (6.3cm) wide and long enough to go right around the quilt, plus about 11in (28cm) to allow for turning the corners and overlapping at the start and finish. Both ends of the binding should be trimmed on the diagonal as in Fig 2 (page 123).

2 Fold and press a ¼in (6mm) seam to the wrong side of one diagonal end of the length of binding (Fig 11). Fold the binding in half lengthwise, right side *outwards*, and press the entire length.

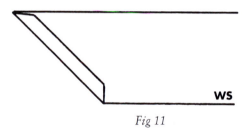

WS

Fig 11

3 Starting with this folded end, pin the folded binding strip along one side of the quilt, matching the edges of the binding with the edge of the quilt top. Do not begin at a corner of the quilt. Instead, make the start and finish of the binding some way down one side where it will be less obvious (Fig 12). Pin to exactly ¼in (6mm) from the nearest corner of the quilt top. Mark this point on the binding with a dot (Fig 13).

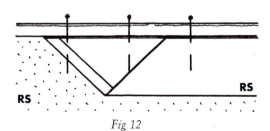

RS

RS

Fig 12

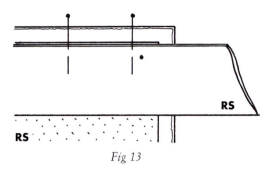

RS

RS

Fig 13

4 Begin stitching 4in–5in (10–12.5cm) from the start of the pinned binding, using a ¼in (6mm) seam allowance. Finish exactly on the marked dot, backstitching to secure the seam.

5 Remove the quilt from the machine and place it on a flat surface ready for pinning the next side. Fold the binding back at right angles from the stitched side (Fig 14).

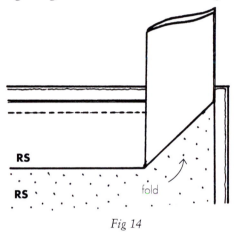

RS

RS

fold

Fig 14

6 Fold the binding down again with the top fold level with the edge of the wadding (batting) and backing and the raw edges level with the edge of the quilt top (Fig 15).

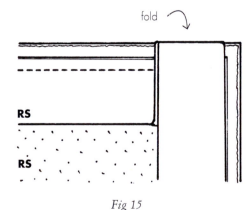

fold

RS

RS

Fig 15

7 Pin the folded layers in place and continue to pin the binding to the side of the quilt until it reaches the next corner. Mark the turning corner ¼in (6mm) from the edge of the quilt top with a dot as before.

8 Stitch the pinned binding with the usual ¼in (6mm) seam, starting at the edge of the quilt (Fig 16) and continuing to the marked dot. Backstitch to secure the seam at the dot.

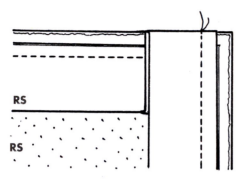

Fig 16

9 Continue to pin and stitch the binding to the quilt, one side at a time, using the method above for turning each corner. On the final side where the binding starts and finishes, slip the finishing end of the strip between the layers of the other end of the binding. Trim it so that the folded edge of the beginning section overlaps the end piece by about ½in (12mm) (Fig 17). Pin the overlapping sections and stitch.

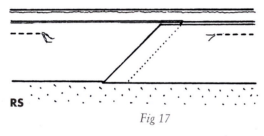

Fig 17

10 Fold the binding over to the back of the quilt and stitch it by hand in the same way as the square-cornered binding. The front corners will form a neat mitre that can be tweaked into place and left unstitched as a diagonal fold (Fig 18). The diagonal overlap where the two ends of binding meet can be left unstitched or made more secure by hand stitching in a matching thread. The corners on the back of the quilt should be arranged into a mitre by folding one side down and then the other side. Arrange the fold in the opposite direction to the fold on the front to distribute the layers evenly and make a flat corner.

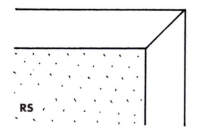

Fig 18

Rulers to Make the Job Easier

Several of the quilt designs in this book can be made more easily and efficiently by using a specialist ruler. These are not cheap, so it is probably not economic to buy one just for one project, but some I find invaluable for everyday quiltmaking. Perhaps several quilters could share one purchase, at least to start with. You need to try these products to find out which ones you find really useful and which you can happily live without. I like to use Creative Grids rulers which all come with detailed instructions on how to use them.

Pineapple Ruler: This ruler eliminates the need for a drawn foundation for every Pineapple block. It is easy to use but can be less accurate than the foundation method. I always use the ruler to make Pineapple blocks and find the best solution to the blocks not measuring exactly the same as each other is to make all the blocks without the final triangular corners. The blocks can then all be trimmed to the same size at this stage before the corners are added.

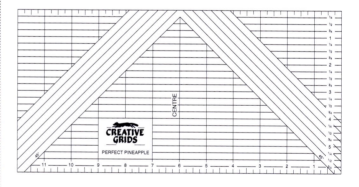

45° Triangle Ruler: With this ruler it is possible to cut two half-square triangles from two layered strips of different fabrics at the same time, ready for stitching in pairs to make squares. The dotted line near the top point of the ruler is used as a marker so that the triangles can be cut from strips that are just ½in (12mm) wider than the finished square instead of the usual ⅞in (2.1cm) which saves fabric and is easier to measure.

60° Triangle Ruler: This ruler is used to cut equilateral triangles of any size from strips rather than using templates. It can also be used to cut the 30° triangles that are needed at either end of the 60° triangles to finish off with a vertical edge. The Magic Lanterns quilts were both made using this ruler.

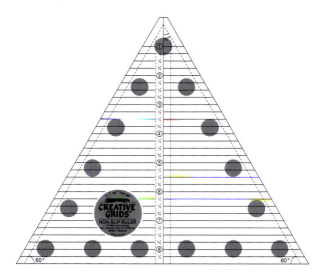

Triangle Duo Ruler: This ruler combines both 45° and 60° rulers, one at either end of the ruler. As it cuts triangles up to 4in (10cm) in height I find it really useful for cutting the half-square triangles for blocks and borders. I used it to make the half-square triangles for the Split Nine-patch quilt on page 51 and was able to use the same width strips of fabric for both the squares and the triangles in the design. I used the 60° end of the ruler for cutting the small equilateral triangles used to make the border on my Magic Lantern quilt (page 35).

Acknowledgments

My thanks to the following people:

To my friends and mentors Barbara Chainey and Pepper Cory for advice and comments given only when sought.

To Cheryl Brown at David & Charles who understood and was patient when I wouldn't write another book until I had something to say.

To Lin Clements for her usual soothing and reasonable support in editing.

To the team at Creative Grids who make it possible for me to cut a straight piece of fabric. Tel: 0845 4507722. www.creativegrids.com

To all the Chelsworth Quilters who made quilts from their left-over fabric in the vain hope that they would actually use it all up. . .

Index